RADIO-TELEVISION AND ELECTIONS

Concept's International Series in Communication Education and Development

INTERNATIONAL ADVISORY BOARD MEMBERS

Concept's International Series in Communication Education and Development—2

General Editor : **Binod C. Agrawal**

RADIO-TELEVISION AND ELECTIONS

DR. P.V. SHARADA

CONCEPT PUBLISHING COMPANY, NEW DELHI 110059

About the Author

Dr. P.V. Sharada is presently working as Programme Executive, All India Radio, Kurnool, Andhra Pradesh. Prior to this, she was a Reader at the Department of Communication, (on deputation) Indian Institute of Health and Family Welfare, Hyderabad where she conducted training, research and communication material production. Before joining the Institute she served All India Radio for sixteen years (1978-94). A science graduate, Sharada holds an M.A. in Philosophy, M.Ed. and Ph.D from Osmania University. She has previously written *Impact of Television on the Political Awareness of Rural Masses* and co-authored *Challenges in Watershed Development.*

ISBN 81-7022-695-3.

First Published 1998

Published and Printed by
Ashok Kumar Mittal
Concept Publishing Company
A/15-16, Commercial Block, Mohan Garden
New Delhi 110059 (India)

Phones: 5648039, 5649024
Fax: 091–(11)–5648053

GENERAL EDITOR'S INTRODUCTION

In India, we have very few research studies related to political communication through electronic media. While there is a great deal of writing by political commentators about democratic process of election, serious studies by communication experts are few. This study provides a first hand glimpse of political communication during mid-term 1991 General Elections to the Lok Sabha in Andhra Pradesh which has had a long spell of single party rule since India's independence.

The study aimed at understanding and analysing the perceptions of political leaders, on various aspects of election campaigning through radio and television. Politicians of Andhra Pradesh State Assembly who were in office at the time of the study, Members of the Rajya Sabha and Lok Sabha, former Union and State Ministers from Andhra Pradesh constituted the universe of the study. About 100 politicians were selected for collecting data using a questionnaire method.

This study provides a detailed analysis of the perceptions of the politicians on diverse subjects. The broad analysis is presented across age and political position of the individual politicians and party lines. The relationships between political attitude and media effects have been examined as also factors influencing political communication processes. In doing so, Dr. Sharada has attempted to develop a suitable model for media coverage of elections. In addition Dr. Sharada has tried to echo minority opinions.

The research study provides an interesting commentary on the government policy to allow political parties to use the electronic media for election campaigns. The politicians are happy with the broadcast timings for political campaigns (incidentally political campaigns were telecast during prime time) but they disfavour equal time to all parties regardless of their political strength in Parliament or Legislative Assembly. At the same time the politicians are dissatisfied with the present broadcasting duration and wanted more time to air their views.

There are sharp differences on the issue of the utility of electronic media as a means of political campaign. This was born out of their political campaign experiences. The regional parties like Telugu Desam considered door-to-door campaigning as the best method and medium of campaign whereas Bharatiya Janata Party thought television was the most important in influencing the voters. On the other hand, the Communist Parties thought it prudent to rely on print medium and press.

Based on years of experience, older politicians favoured press and print medium more than the younger politicians who preferred TV as they thought it was the most influential in changing the attitude and behaviour. On the whole print medium followed by television seemed to be the single most important means of communication for political campaign.

The real value of this book lies in its effort to bring political campaign and the resultant influence on voters in the realm of empirical research. It is for this reason that it was thought most important to bring out this book in this series. Our effort is to encourage research in communication. Hence this is a valuable addition and effort. It will also encourage communication research in India apart from providing base line data for future research.

Binod C. Agrawal
General Editor

PREFACE

Political communication is an area of specialisation drawing the attention of researchers. While development of television has enriched the field, elections particularly have strengthened the methodology providing scope for the use of both qualitative and quantitative measurement techniques. The effects of political broadcasting are extensively explored elsewhere in the world whereas in India the research is not much significant. Journalists, Politicians and Audience are the main participants in political communication process. However, the available research in this area has mainly focussed on the audience especially changing the attitudes of voters. Much less is talked about the others particularly politicians. The present study identified this group as key persons and sought their opinions on election campaigning through Radio and Television.

Content and technique are the two major components of a programme on media. An effective election broadcast demands the politicians to have good knowledge about their subject and understanding of strengths and weaknesses of electronic media. The increasing awareness of politicians about the use of Radio and Television as political instruments also demands new skills to use them in a meaningful manner. The present study made an attempt in this direction to assess the levels of knowledge and understanding of different party leaders about party—political broadcasts. Radio and Television provide opportunity to contenders to broadcast during elections. Due to this and also in view of the intensive campaigning activity before polls elections were felt as the most suitable time to assess the perceptions of leaders about using Radio and Television as election tools.

The present work is a report based on an empirical study. The analysis of responses particularly about the production techniques in election broadcasts and also the voting models and different approaches to media coverage of elections may be of some interest to broadcasters.

Dr. P.V. Sharada

ACKNOWLEDGEMENTS

I am deeply indebted to late Dr. J.S. Murthy Department of Genetics, Osmania University, Hyderabad for providing valuable guidance throughout the study. His vast experience and expertise as researcher, positive thinking and intelligent criticism have immensely helped me in producing this report.

I am grateful to Dr. T.C.A. Srinivasa Ramanujan IAS the then Director General National Institute of Rural Development, Hyderabad for sparing some of his precious time to read the manuscript and offer comments.

A special word of thanks is due to Dr. Usha Vyasula Reddy, Director, Audio Visual Research Centre, Hyderabad for the critical review of the book and the valid suggestions offered. My profound thanks to Dr. Binod C. Agarwal Director Taleem Research Foundation, Ahmedabad, India for the General Editer's Introduction to the book.

I am highly thankful to all the distinguished political leaders for their excellent co-operation in responding to the interviews and discussing the subject with interest amidst hectic election campaigning. The interaction has been highly enlightening and provided basic data for the study.

I am thankful to my husband Sri J. Sai Kumar for his unstinted co-operation throughout the project. Without his support, encouragement and help it would have not been possible to accomplish this book.

I feel indebted to my parents and children for bearing all the inconveniences caused in carrying out the work.

Mr. Thomas deserves warm appreciation for his help in neatly typing the manuscript. Lastly, sincere thanks are due to all my friends who helped in collecting the basic data.

Dr. P.V. Sharada

CONTENTS

	General Editor's Introduction	v
	Preface	vii
	Acknowledgements	ix
	List of Tables	xii
1.	Introduction	1
2.	Review of Previous Literature	5
3.	Methodology	11
4.	Present Broadcasts : Merits and Demerits	21
5.	Multi-media Campaign	33
6.	Conceptions about the Audience	51
7.	Improvements in the Present Set-up	66
8.	Some Perceptions about Broadcast Media and Politics	96
9.	Political Attitudes : Effects of Media	121
10.	Media Coverage of Elections (Voting Models and Agenda Setting Approaches)	140
11.	Summary/Conclusions	153
	Questionnaire	166
	Bibliography	176
	Index	179

LIST OF TABLES

Table No.	Details	P. No.
4.1	Distribution of responses whether the leaders were satisfied with the quantum of party broadcasts (Q. No. 3)	22
4.2	Distribution of preferred frequency of party broadcasts (Q. No. 3a)	22
4.3	Distribution of ideal duration of party broadcasts preferred by leaders (Q. No. 3)	23
4.4	Distribution of responses whether the leaders were satisfied with the timings of party broadcasts (Q. No. 4)	24
4.5	Distribution of responses whether equal opportunity could be extended to all political parties (Q. No. 5)	25
4.6	Distribution of responses whether enough freedom of expression is given in party broadcasts (Q. No. 6)	27
4.7	Distribution of responses on the desirability of election code for party broadcasts (Q. No. 7)	28
4.8	Distribution of preferences on who should formulate the code (Q. No. 7a)	29
4.9	Distribution of responses on the need for editing the script in party broadcasts (Q. No. 8)	30
4.10	Distribution of responses on the type of offences that may be allowed in party broadcasts (Q. No. 8a)	31
5.1.	Distribution of responses on the most influencing media unit (Q. No. 1)	35

5.2 Distribution of preferences for party broadcasts (Q. No. 9) 38

5.3. Distribution of reasons for film personalities winning more votes (Q. No. 13) 40

5.4. Distribution of responses on the use of Audio and Video cassettes during elections (Q. No. 14) 43

5.5. Distribution of responses on the role of local Radios in future politics (Q. No. 38) 44

5.6. Distribution of responses on the extent of local Radio's role in future politics (Q. No. 38a) 44

5.7 Distribution of responses on the choice of medium for promoting future political career (Q. No. 37) 46

6.1. Distribution of responses on the knowledgeability of rural folk in appreciating media campaigning (Q. No. 17) 52

6.2. Distribution of responses on the impact of intensity of viewing of party broadcasts by the audience/voters (Q. No. 18) 53

6.3. Distribution of responses on the type of audience showing more interest in party broadcasts (Q. No. 19) 55

6.4. Distribution of responses on men of different categories affected by the party broadcasts (Q. No. 20) 57

6.5. Distribution of responses on women of different categories showing interest in party broadcasts (Q. No. 20a) 58

6.6. Distribution of responses as per rural-urban background of voters that respond more positively to political messages (Q. No. 21) 59

7.1. Distribution of responses on giving opportunity to unrecognised political parties and independents in party broadcasts (Q. No. 23) 68

7.2. Distribution of responses on the formats for party broadcasts (Q. No. 24) 70
7.3. Distribution of responses on the need for giving prominence for party symbol in party broadcasts (Q. No. 25) 75
7.4. Distribution of responses on the effectiveness of political advertizement (Q. No. 26) 76
7.5. Distribution of responses on the use of visuals and films in party broadcasts (Q. No. 27) 79
7.6. Distribution of responses as to whether the future party broadcasts to be followed by experts' analysis (Q. No. 39) 82
7.7. Distribution of responses on the type of analysis for party broadcasts (Q. No. 39) 83
7.8. Distribution of agencies whose guidance is sought before giving party broadcasts (Q. No. 10) 87
7.9. Distribution of responses on the selection of person for party broadcasts (Q. No. 11) 90
7.10 Distribution of responses on the extent of empty promises made in election broadcasts (Q. No. 15) 93
8.1 Distribution of Responses on the Type of the types of learning promoted by Broadcast media (Q. No. 28) 98
8.2 Distribution of responses whether party broadcasts reach voters in difficult segments (Q. No. 29) 101
8.3 Distribution of responses whether party broadcasts are promoting discussion in the homes (Q. No. 30) 103
8.4 Distribution of responses whether party broadcasts maintain neutrality (Q. No. 31) 105
8.5 Distribution of responses whether Television gives publicity boost to less established contenders (Q. No. 32) 108

8.6. Distribution of responses on the impact of political unsophistication on the broadcast media campaigning (Q. No. 33) 110
8.7. Distribution of responses on the effect of political accusations on the minds of audience (Q. No. 34) 113
8.8. Distribution of responses as to what extent empty promises would damage the credibility of broadcast media (Q. No. 35) 115
8.9. Distribution of responses as to whether the non-fulfilment of promises would lead to frustration amongst rural voters (Q. No. 36) 116
9.1. Distribution of responses on the influence of pre-election broadcasts on the voters in the past (Q. No. 2) 123
9.2. Distribution of responses on the impact of pre-election broadcasts on the audience voters (Q. No. 16) 124
9.3. Distribution of responses on the influence of Radio/TV on the most deep-seated political attitudes of the voters in future (Q. No. 40) 125
9.4 Distribution of factors influencing the voter's party (Q. No. 12) 129
9.5. Distribution of factors influencing the voters-candidate (Q. No. 12) 131
9.6. Distribution of factors influencing the voters (Q. No. 12) 133
9.7. Distribution of factors determining the voting pattern (Q. No. 22) 135
9.8. Distribution of responses whether the politicians listen/watch to the other party broadcasts (Q. No. 41) 137

Chapter 1

INTRODUCTION

Radio and Television which constitute the main communication media, have made a tremendous impact in recent years in spreading knowledge and providing entertainment. They are now playing an active role in the field of po`litics too. The Second world war, was the major catalyst for the invasion of Radio and Television network into politics in many parts of the world; but the role of Broadcast media in Indian politics was insignificant even till recently. For a long time entertainment dominated the media and it is only with the passage of time that people began to realise the hard realities of the world around and of politics in particular through these media.

Elections have occupied a special role in the field of media and politics. The prime objective of a politician is to win elections. As Blumler[1] observes "An election is a special, infrequent, yet in a sense quite decisive event, in which voters are invited to choose between political alternatives laid before them. It unleashes a more ample flood of overtly political materials on to the heads of citizens than they are expected to cope with at any other moment of the civic calendar". Political communication research has also so far concentrated mostly on this area of elections.

Election campaigning is another important aspect. A close relationship can be seen between mass media and election campaigning especially at a national level. Quoting Butler and Stokes Ure[2] explains three different types of election campaigns : (1) Campaigning through informal discussions with family and friends. (2) Local party workers holding public meetings, etc., and giving publicity to their party and the candidate. (3) National campaign of the party leaders through election broadcasts, press conferences and platform speeches. Mass media contribute to all these types of campaigning by providing information to the candidates and by carrying messages that reflect their opinion about the parties. But the national campaign is determined and formed by a continuous interaction between the behaviour of party leaders and managers and that of the masses".

Why do campaigning and elections occupy a significant place in political communication? Quoting Lazarsfeld Blumler[3] further observes :

> "arguments enter the final stage of decision (of voters) more as indicators than as influences. They point out, like sign boards along the road, the way to turn in order to reach a destination which is already predetermined. The political predispositions and group allegiances set the goal, all that is read and heard becomes helpful and effective in so far as it guides the voter towards his already chosen destination. The clinching arguments thus do not have the function of persuading the voter to act. He furnishes the motive power himself. The argument has the function of identifying for him the way of thinking and acting which he is already half aware of wanting".

Elections are often compared with horse races given the unpredictable developments that take place during the time. But there is also a feeling that media coverage of election campaigning creates such an impression. One of the chief criticisms of media's performance during elections, Gamble and Gamble[4] say, is their tendency to treat them as horse race. "By far more attention is paid to questions such as who is ahead, who is fading and what strategies are being used than to the substantive issues of the day. Another aspect of the horse race mentality is their tendency to label one candidate as the front-runner and the others as underdogs. If a so called underdog then performs better than the expected, the press often shifts attention from the old front runner and starts treating the new one as a winner. Most members of the press like to see this happen because it adds excitement to the campaign coverage".

However, mass media are vital to democratic elections whether the coverage is through Radio/TV or press; and campaigning is the most crucial phase of an election where the contender is an important person.

Much research has been carried out on Broadcast media and politics. What is the role of political communication in influencing the voters' decision? What is the basis for judging the competence of a party, leader or candidate to govern the people? Why do political parties show interest in media campaigning? The emergence of such questions brought the subject into lime light. The importance is further strengthened by the role of Television during the Presidential elections in U.S.A., but the discussions are still under debate at various levels. Till now the available research has mainly concentrated on the audience's point of view. Not much thought has been given to the effects of mass-media on voting behaviour from the politicians' angle.

Majority of the political parties today are quite inclined for electronic campaigning. They have even come to a stage of arguing about the insufficient time allotted to them. A hue and cry is raised for autonomy for AIR and Doordarshan (a common point in almost all the election manifestos). None-the-less many aspects are not clear. What are their real motives? Their preferences in the presentation of party broadcasts? The extent of faith they hold about the effect of media campaigning on their target audience i.e. voters? Do they have a clear picture about the target group? Are they of the conviction that electronic campaigning will benefit them more than the other modes available? What are their efforts before giving a party broadcast? These are but some of the questions which need to be answered before assessing the precise achievement and influence of electronic campaigning. Hence, the present study has been designed to assess the perspectives of 100 politicians involved in the thick of an election campaign on party propaganda through Radio and Television, figuratively, thus from the horses in the race.

REFERENCES

1. Blumler, J.G., *The Political Effects of Mass Communication*; The Audience Unit 8, The Open University Social Sciences a third level course, Milton Keyness Walton Hall : p. 13.
2. Ure, C.S., *The Political Impact of Mass Media*, London Constable & Co., : p. 24.
3. Blumler, J.G. *op.cit*, p. 16.
4. Gamble, Michael W. and Gamble, Teri Kwal; *Introducing Mass Communication*—Singapore McGraw Hill Book Co., 1989 pp. 400 and 401.

Chapter 2

REVIEW OF PREVIOUS LITERATURE

The following are the few relevant studies conducted on the effects of electronic media on voters during elections. While the analysis and findings of research done outside India is extensively used in the forthcoming chapters wherever found suitable the present discussion is limited to studies conducted only in India to enable to assess the situation well. Studies that explored different areas of political communications are many. Among them a few which concentrated more on electronic media and elections were selected for presentation.

An intensive study of the communication process at village level was undertaken during the Lok Sabha elections in 1971 with the following objectives in view.[1]

1. To document all the communication events that take place during the election period in and around a village,
2. To study the total inflow of information about the election into the village, and
3. To investigate the channels and mechanism of spread of information within the villages.

Mandothi, a village in Haryana, formed the focus of the study.

The sample study in the village revealed that the majority of the respondents first came to know the news about the forthcoming elections mainly through public meetings, party propaganda, and their kinsmen and friends in the village. Mass media, Radio, and Newspapers were of lesser significance in this regard. However, comparatively speaking, the persons belonging to the upper castes and having education, first received the news more often through the Radio than the lower castes and the Harijans and, illiterate respondents came to know about it mainly through party propaganda, kinsmen and friends.

Further it was found that the respondents were exposed to the election propaganda mainly through the public meetings. The majority (75.5%) of the respondents attended atleast one public meeting. Moreover, exposure to public meetings seemed to have induced the respondents to attend other sources of election information also.

As part of the Satellite Instructional Television Experiment (SITE) an effort was made to measure the gain in political information, empathy, National Integration and views regarding administrative efficacy and overall political socialization.[2] It was found that there was a statistically significant difference in the gains of the TV viewers over the control group. On the question of empathy, the hypothesis was that with exposure to television, people would be able to empathize with the different roles and it was found that the hypothesis was supported. Both male and female viewers gained significantly over the control group in empathy. On National Integration, it was found that there was a significant gain here also when one takes the political socialisation area as a whole inclusive of all the various subareas. One finds that only the frequent viewers had changed in a positive direction in large measure compared to the control group. The relatively lower gain of illiterate female frequent viewers indicated that rural Indian women were perhaps by and large not interested in politics.

The greater gain in political socialization among illiterate males suggests that Television and Audio-visual media can be effective despite lack of formal education.

Audience research unit of Delhi Doordarshan has conducted a survey to study the impact of political broadcasts on TV[3]. It covered both urban and rural areas. A three phase model was used. A fixed sample of respondents were interviewed before and after telecast as well as during the telecast period. The survey was conducted at the time of 1980 Lok Sabha elections.

The report of the study says that a good majority of the respondents found the telecast to be useful. A majority of the viewers marked the utility of such telecasts in terms of clarification of parties' programmes and policies. To some, such telecasts provided political education. Listening to these broadcasts was considerable in both the rural and urban areas. The response regarding the practical utility of these broadcasts were as follows:

- helped to identify programme and policies of various political parties.
- enabled to listen to the voices of the leaders.
- reached the illiterate masses.
- created political consciousness among the people.
- saved time and money for both the voters and the politicians.

Uma Narula presents the results of a research study done by Indian Institute of Mass Communication on the trends of the recent elections in India which reveals the existence of a variety of variables and complexities that guided voting decisions and behaviour of masses[4]. In examining the role of communication channels the agenda setting role and interpersonal communication channels play a significant role in election process. Though the Indian press has played a negligible role in the education and participatory involvement of the masses in political communication it has always played a significant role in directing the public thinking to poll considerations. These considerations include caste, creed, regional biases, hero worship, particular sympathy waves and familial ties etc.

J. S. Yadava's study is based on analysis of data collected in a nation-wide study of the election campaign during the eighth parliamentary elections held in December, 1984[5]. The main focus of the study was on media coverage campaign material and the audience reactions. The theoretical consideration here was that the election campaign helps in reinforcing and mobilizing the opinions of the electorate and not so much converting them. He says that during a period of 18 to 24 months preceding the elections the mass media serve to place the current issues of politics on the agenda of citizens discussions. Through the interplay of mass-media and interpersonal communication, the essence of major political issues gets disseminated widely among the electorate even among illiterates and those living in remote areas. As a result they form their impressions and opinions about leaders and parties. During the election campaign, the contending parties and candidates try to consolidate such impressions and opinions about selected political issues in the form of their major election themes and appeals so as to convert them into actual voting in their favour as opposed to their opponents. The campaign heightens the interest of the voters in public affairs. But the voters selectively expose themselves to election information and appeals. They invariably read more news about their respective favourite political parties and leaders. They will pay greater attention to the arguments supporting their already favourite leaders, whether they are in the press, posters, public meetings or advertisements. The result is largely reinforcement and mobilisation and not much change in inclinations and opinions as such.

To this end Dr. Yadava closely observed the so called political advertising and campaign procedures adopted by each party before the elections. Dr. Yadava made an in-depth observation of how much publicity material like print, electronic media, especially audio and visual cassettes were used to gain the attention of the electorate. A notable observation in the study is the consideration of prevailing mental and emotional atmosphere in the country during that period. He noted that campaigns were carried on by some parties, without any cost consideration whereas some other parties which could not compete due to lack of funds were able to make only limited use of the available modern techniques of persuasion. In his conclusion Dr. Yadava implies that effective campaigning although does not get totally accepted by the voters, it certainly helps in reinforcing the impressions and opinions that already exist in the minds of the voters.

A study about the impact of Television on Rural Masses with reference to their levels of political awareness by the author of the present work has discussed the opinions of Rural audience about pre-election broadcasts, as a part of the study[6]. It was observed, though the rural voters have realised the importance of these broadcasts their final decision as to whom to vote is not entirely based on the programmes. Villagers watch these broadcasts just to know what is being said by different political parties.

As the few studies mentioned above speaks, the research as such conducted in election communication is very limited and mostly represents the audience perspective. The Audience Research Units of All India Radio and Doordarshan usually conduct feedback studies after broadcasts during election period. But their purpose is limited. The scope and potential for research in this area is tremendous and especially with the opening of private channels much can be anticipated in future.

REFERENCES

1. Yadava J.S., *Communication and Parliamentary Election* (1971), *A Study in Haryana Village*, Department of Research, Indian Institute of Mass Communication, New Delhi.
2. The SITE Experience, Reports and Papers on Mass Communication, No. 91, UNESCO, Paris 1983, p. 179.
3. Baruah, U.L., This is All India Radio-Publications Division, Ministry of Information and Broadcasting, New Delhi, 1983 p. 179.
4. Uma Narula, Electorate Choice : A Process of Communication—Communicator, Jan 85, *Quarterly Journal of the Indian Institute of Mass-Communication* Vol, XX, No. 1, New Delhi, pp. 24-25.
5. Yadava, J.S., Campaign and Voters Choice, 1984, Parliamentary Elections, *Communicator,* Jan 85, Indian Institute of Mass-Communication, New Delhi, pp. 18-23.
6. Sharada, P.V., *Impact of Television on the Political Awareness of the Rural Masses*, 1991, Gyan Publishing House, New Delhi, pp. 174.

Chapter 3

METHODOLOGY

Election Broadcasts—Present Position

In India, party political broadcasting is of a recent origin. TV and Radio are providing the different political parties to broadcast on the eve of elections. As Baruah[1] observes, "The proposals made by the Election Commission in 1962 gave each national party fifteen minutes with an additional 15 minutes for the ruling Congress party. The Election Commission made similar efforts in 1967 and 1971 but failed. The Janata party government decided in May 1977 that facilities for broadcasting should be provided equally to National and Regional parties on the eve of State Assembly elections in June 1977. Each political party recognized by the Election Commission and given an election symbol under Election symbols (Reservation and Allotment) Act 1968 was given equal opportunity to broadcast from the broadcasting stations in the states concerned for the first time when elections to state assemblies were held in ten states and two union territories in June 1977. Broadcast facilities were given to all the National and regional parties contesting the elections, from all the Radio and TV stations located in the state. There were two rounds of broadcast of a duration of fifteen minutes each by each political party on Radio and one on TV. The schedule of broadcasts was drawn up by lots by Station Directors located at state capitals in the presence of the Chief Electoral Officer and the representatives of political parties. The language of the broadcasts and names of the speakers were decided by the respective political parties. Independent candidates challenged these broadcasts as discriminatory. However, the courts did not uphold these. Broadcasts were prerecorded usually at the state capitals and copies of tapes were sent to all stations in the state in order to ensure an uninterrupted broadcast".

In the three general elections to the Indian Parliament, Radio and TV broadcast facilities were made available to all the recognised national and regional parties contesting the elections. It is, however, not clear whether the perceptions as held by the media researchers are shared by the politicians or whether their current enthusiasm for propaganda through electronic media is only a sign of vanity and a cheap imitation of the Western scenario. The present study has, therefore, been taken up to examine the perceptions of politicians, as a study group, about the electronic campaigning i.e., on party broadcasts over Radio and Television in the context of Indian voters' mysterious but decidedly pragmatic behaviour.

Objectives

Major Objective

To study the effectiveness of Radio and Television as election media from a politician's perspective.

Minor Objectives

(1) To know the politicians'
- (a) Opinions about the present Programmes--merits and demerits,
- (b) Conceptions about Audience (Voters),
- (c) Knowledge about multi-media campaigning,
- (d) Suggestions for improvements in the present set-up,

   (e) Perceptions about the role of broadcast media in politics etc.

(2) To see the influence of variables such as age, position etc. on their perceptions.

(3) To study the relation between political attitudes and Media effects, and factors influencing political communication process.

(4) To study the existing voting models and communication methods and develop suitable models for the media coverage of elections.

Sample

Since the politicians are the target group of the study, as many as 100 politicians were taken as the sample, which included the Chief Minister, Ex-Union Information and Broadcasting Minister, and Speaker and Deputy Speaker of the Andhra Pradesh State Assembly, who were in office at the time of the study. Others who made the group were Ministers and Ex-ministers of Central and state government, M.Ps and Ex-M.Ps (both Lok Sabha and Rajya Sabha), M.L.As. and M.L.Cs. (both present and former), party workers and other political thinkers and activists. Preference was given to senior and active politicians. Considering the strength of the parties and their political ideologies, it was decided to select 50 members from Congress (I), 25 from Telugu Desam Party (TDP), 10 each from Bharatiya Janata Party (BJP) and Communist Parties (CPI, CIP (M) & MCPI put together) and 5 others.

Elections are unique opportunities for the political communication researchers for probing and testing various theories. The present study was conducted during the General Election to the Lok Sabha in 1991. Announcement of the Midterm poll to be held in April 1991, due to the dissolution of Parliament in February 1991, helped the politicians to utilise the facility of electronic media campaigning, a free service offered by the Government to the parties. They welcomed party broadcasts to strengthen their canvassing.

The neutral voters who sometimes reverse/turn the fate of the political parties, count much to the campaigners. Politicians mostly depend on media to impress these wobblers/floaters. As Ure[2] opines "elections make politicians pay attention to what people think". Notwithstanding the forecasts based on opinion polls and surveys they find it difficult to understand a voter's mind, especially the neutral voters. The hectic political activity revolving round the aspirations of the contenders, issues at stake, the persuasion process etc. create a sort of fever among the people and the politicians alike.

This atmosphere obtained during the parliamentary elections of April-June 1991 was felt as the proper time to know the opinions and perceptions of the politicians about the Broadcast media campaigning especially before the election results are announced as the outcome may sometimes influence the opinions of the sample. This has posed some problems to the researcher since most of the candidates were engaged in campaigning at their respective constituencies and unable to spare time for a detailed research study. The Prime Minister Shri Rajiv Gandhi's assassination also has some effect on the situation as the elections were postponed by 3 to 4 weeks. The politicians were forced to change their election strategies and apply much thought to the campaigning, keeping the new circumstances, mood of the voters and the possibilities of electoral turnout in view.

Politics and politicians are treated with some apathy in our country though they may form an interesting subject over a cup of tea for many. It is, therefore, to be greatly appreciated that almost all the respondents of the study readily consented for the interview on the questionnaire sent to them and plunged themselves into the subject during the discussion. The study has also provided the researcher a thrilling experience of visiting rival camps in the battlefield. While answering some of the questions they were emotional and criticized the mode and means of campaigning adopted by other parties. This was more so with Congress (I) and TDP as these two were the major parties, one in power and the other hoping to regain power in the State. (At the time of publishing this study the TDP is voted to power in AP).

Tools

For the purpose of collecting the required data, a detailed questionnaire was administered on the sample. The questionnaire was divided into 5 parts. The first part was an attempt to know the sample's opinion on the state of the present party broadcasts, their merits and demerits. While the second part sought to observe their conception about the audience, the third invited their suggestions for improvements in the present set-up. Some general perceptions about the broadcast media and politics were dealt in the fourth part. The final part concentrated on future expectations. Questions pertaining to certain related aspects of the study were also included in the schedule without which the discussion about the role of Broadcast media as a vehicle of party propaganda may not be complete.

It is generally agreed that in any opinion oriented research, personal discussions with the sample would be of much help in gaining indepth knowledge of the target group in the subject concerned. So, in addition to sending the questionnaire, the researcher felt it desirable and to some extent necessary to have personal discussions with the sample group while seeking their answers to the questionnaire. It was observed that the politicians found the first, third and last sections of the questionnaire interesting since the items were directly related to their field experience. While answering the second and fourth parts, the representatives felt a bit of strain to go into the academic aspect of the electioneering through media. However, vast experience and maturity seem to have helped them in responding with confidence to the enquiries.

In India, the political programme output over Radio and Television is not intensive enough to study each medium separately. Especially, Television is not within reach of common man. Hence, though there is a considerable difference between the two media, keeping their similarity at conceptual level and due to the other constraints, Radio and Television have been studied together and the questionnaire has been prepared accordingly.

Questions consisted of both multiple choice and graded response types. Responses to the multiple choice questions were grouped and presented as frequencies and percentages. The responses for different questions are presented partywise in different tables. In case of questions where the respondents were required to give scores or order of preference, the mean scores were calculated. For this purpose, the responses were multiplied by the scores given to them and the totals of the same were divided by the respective frequency totals.

The perceptions based on responses were analysed subject-wise and party-wise. Certain minority responses which have shown unusual nature were also highlighted. The influence of variables like age and position of the politicians on the response, was identified and discussed.

Analysis of Data

Party-wise Analysis

An aphorism by H.L. Mencker quoted by Cartwright[3] is, "under democracy, one party always devotes its chief energy to trying to prove that the other party is unfit to rule. Both commonly succeed and are right". Party ideology is an important aspect in the democratic system of politics. It is reflected in the stances parties take on different issues. Regarding electronic media also parties differ in their perspective. Only recently, political parties have started discussing about media as a major subject. This was also not an important issue on which parties were normally concerned.

The recent public debate (1991) at various platforms over autonomy to Broadcast media generated some thought among the parties about the stand they have to take on this issue, which still has to take a concrete shape. So much so some Party-wise difference of opinion was noticed in the responses though not similar in all the items. The reason for these difference can be attributed to party ideology to some extent. However, some deviations did not exactly represent the respective party's policies or programmes but only reflected the individual opinions of the respondents.

In a party system, politicians have certain restrictions in the name of discipline. When their party supports or opposes an issue they have to go by the party decision, which is usually a majority decision irrespective of the personal opinion they hold. Even though the politicians did not experience this problem in the present study, the responses did show shades of party ideology in quite some areas.

Minority Responses

In an opinion analysis the conventional practice is to attach importance to majority opinions. But at times unexpected minor responses also convey some valid points. It is also observed that while majority represents common knowledge minority responses occasionally provide new dimension of thought irrespective of their feasibility in implementation. The present study has noticed some such responses. It was felt that an examination of these responses may add further information to the understanding of the subject under discussion. Some individual opinions expressed by the sample (some of which do not fit conveniently into the responses provided in the questionnaire) are felt worthy of note and would make valid contribution to the improvement and effective implementation of party broadcasts. Hence they were also presented in the analysis.

Influence of Age and Position on the Responses

Analysis of any study in social sciences cannot be deemed complete without considering the influence of variables like sex, age, education etc. of the subjects. In the present study, the sample being politicians and the subject, their opinion about electronic media campaigning, variables related to socio-economic background like caste, religion of the politicians, may not have much relevance to their opinions. However, age and political experience may to some extent influence the responses. It is generally felt that maturity increases with age making a person more rational and balanced in his opinion and ideas. Similar is the case with experience. In politics, this experience is of two kinds. One, the period spent in the field and the other the period of holding responsible positions in Government and official machinery, i.e. Ministry etc. Compared to a politician who spent all his service in opposition parties, a leader who served as minister perhaps may have more practical knowledge about the affairs of the Government.

With these assumptions the data was analysed by age and position (minister, non-minister) of the respondents. An important observation from this analysis is that in case of majority responses (first preference) the influence was not much except in a few areas; but for second and third preferences the difference was more perceptible in some areas. Although the effect of these two variables was generally not very high, age seems to have more effect than position and some valid conclusions could be drawn from the noticed influence. These aspects as also the possible reason for the influence are discussed. Three age groups i.e. below 45 years (group I), between 45 and 55 years (group II) and above 55 years (group III) were considered for the analysis. In politics, a person below 45 years is usually considered to be young.

The sample consisted mainly two types of politicians. Some were part of the ministry (present or past) and others though in politics for a long period were never a part of the government machinery. The latter category especially includes the MPs and MLAs belonging to the opposition like BJP and Communist Parties. Party workers (with or without position) also were brought under this group. The experience of people who held position in the government for considerable time was recognised as an important factor. While assessing the impact, it was felt that this group cannot be equated with others who did not have such practical knowledge, thus the position of a leader was identified as a potential variable in influencing the responses, and the respondents have been divided into two categories Ministers (group I) and non-ministers (group II).

In addition to the above, the analysis also included discussion on the role of various media units in contributing to the political knowledge of voters during elections, important theories on media coverage of election, and a few models of voting pattern and their relationship to mass media etc.

REFERENCES

1. Baruah, U.L., This is All India Radio; Publications Division, Ministry of Information and Broadcasting; New Delhi, p. 179.
2. Ure, C.S., *The Political Impact of Mass-Media*, London, Constable & Co.
3. Crewe, Ivor and Harrop, Martin, (Ed.) *Political Communications, The General Election Campaign of 1983*, Cambridge, Cambridge University Press, 1986.

Chapter 4

PRESENT PARTY BROADCASTS : MERITS AND DEMERITS

Broadcast facilities are provided to the political parties during elections twice over All India Radio and once on the television network. Recognized parties have been utilizing this facility for quite some time and electronic media campaigning is not a new experience to our leaders. Though they generally abide by the rules and guidelines political parties express varied opinions at every election time as to the election code, freedom of expression, time allotted etc.

To know what exactly the representatives feel about the present system and how far they are able to appreciate it some questions in the first part of the current study refer to the existing broadcast practice i.e. policy guidelines etc.

Frequency of Party Broadcasts

In respect of the quantum of party broadcasts over Radio/TV i.e. once over TV and twice over Radio, the leaders (75%) expressed dissatisfaction (see Table No. 4.1). Nonetheless a considerable number (74.71%) suggested once a weak as the ideal frequency followed by those opting for twice a week (20.71%) (Table 4.2).

Politicians between 45-55 years were not as satisfied as others about the quantum of party broadcasts over Radio/TV. Regarding frequency also this age group gave more score to 'once a week' compared to others. However ministerial position did not make any difference in the opinion.

TABLE NO. 4.1 : **Distribution of Responses whether the Leaders were satisfied with the Quantum of Party Broadcasts (Q. No. 3).**

Party		*Yes*	*No*	*Total*
Congress (I)	Fre	15	35	50
	%	30	70	—
T.D.P.	Fre	6	19	25
	%	24	76	—
B.J.P.	Fre	—	10	10
	%	—	100	—
Communist	Fre	2	8	10
	%	20	80	—
Others	Fre	2	3	5
	%	40	60	—
Total	%	25	75	100

TABLE NO. 4.2 : **Distribution of Preferred Frequency of Party Broadcasts (Q. No. 3a).**

Party		*Once a week*	*Once a fortnight*	*Twice*	*Once*	*Total*
Congress (I)	Fre	30	—	9	—	39
	%	76.92	—	23.07	—	—
T.D.P.	Fre	19	1	1	1	22
	%	86.36	4.54	4.54	4.54	—
B.J.P.	Fre	6	—	4	—	10
	%	60	—	40	—	—
Communist	Fre	4	2	2	—	8
	%	50	25	25	—	—
Others	Fre	2	—	1	—	3
	%	66.66	—	33.33	—	—
Total	Fre	61	3	17	1	82
	%	74.39	3.65	20.73	1.21	100

An examination of individual opinions expressed by the sample has revealed some interesting observations in this aspect, to the effect that party broadcasts should be made a regular programme rather than being a feature only during the elections. A repeated and emphatic suggestion is that it must be a daily affair if not, atleast every alternate day from the date of announcement of election process suspending if necessary some of the regular schedule. A senior politician who served in many responsible positions even opined that party broadcasts should be a daily programme for about an hour in the morning and two to three in the evening. If possible a separate channel may be opened under a caption like 'The democratic forum' preferably under the guidance of a moderator. Supporting the above idea one of the representatives felt that public opinion will not be formed unless the programmes are presented frequently. At a less intense level, is the suggestion of a respondent that a second round opportunity should be provided on TV also at par with the Radio.

Duration

Regarding the duration of the party broadcasts a significant group (37%) preferred 10 to 15 minutes followed by 20 to 30 minutes as ideal duration by a small group (24%) (Table No. 4.3). Congress (I) gave second preference for 15 to 20 minutes duration.

TABLE NO. 4.3 : **Distribution of Ideal Duration of Party Broadcasts Preferred by Leaders (Q. No. 3b)**

Party		*More than 30 Mts*	*20-30 mts.*	*15-20 mts.*	*10-15 mts*	*5-10 mts.*	*Total mts.*
Congress (I)	Fre	2	7	12	18	11	50
	%	4	14	24	36	22	—
T.D.P.	Fre	—	6	5	10	4	25
	%	—	24	20	40	16	—
B.J.P.	Fre	—	6	2	2	—	10
	%	—	60	20	20	—	—
Communist	Fre	—	4	1	5	—	10
	%	—	40	10	50	—	—
Others	Fre	—	1	2	2	—	5
	%	—	20	40	40	—	—
Total	%	2	24	22	37	15	100

Agewise analysis shows that youngsters desired an increase in the duration i.e. 20 to 30 minutes giving second highest score compared to others. Here also ministerial position did not alter their opinions.

Timings of Broadcasts

It is noteworthy that more than 80% of the politicians expressed great satisfaction over the present timings of party broadcasts (Table No. 4.4)

While majority of the first and the last age groups constitute this percentage 26.3% of the middle aged group wanted a shift in the timings.

TABLE NO. 4.4 : **Distribution of Responses whether the Leaders were satisfied with the Timings of Party Broadcasts (Q. No. 4).**

Party		*Yes*	*No*	*Total*
Congress (I)	Fre	39	11	50
	%	78	22	—
T.D.P.	Fre	21	2	23
	%	91.30	8.69	—
B.J.P.	Fre	8	2	10
	%	80	20	—
Communist	Fre	8	1	9
	%	88.8	11.1	—
Others	Fre	4	1	5
	%	80	20	—
Total	Fre	80	17	97
	%	82.47	17.52	100

Opportunity and Time to Different Parties

The next item in the questionnaire was framed to know the sample's views on whether the present system of allocating equal opportunity and time to both big and small parties is reasonable or not. Majority gave a favourable response (68%, Table No. 4.5), but difference of opinion was observed partywise. The ruling Congress (I) (60%) and the opposition TDP (72%) felt the allocation to be reasonable while the

BJP was not content. Communists expressed cent per cent satisfaction. Among others (32%) who felt it unreasonable suggested that the allotment of time should be based on the percentage of votes gained in the last one or two elections or on the basis of the strength in Assembly or Parliament. Another suggestion was that the national parties may be given more time than the regional.

TABLE NO. 4.5 : **Distribution of Responses whether Equal Opportunity could be Extended to all Political Parties. (Q. No. 5)**

Party		*Yes*	*No*	*Total*
Congress (I)	Fre	30	20	50
	%	60	40	—
T.D.P.	Fre	18	7	25
	%	72	28	—
B.J.P.	Fre	6	4	10
	%	60	40	—
Communist	Fre	10	-	10
	%	100	-	—
Others	Fre	4	1	5
	%	80	20	—
Total	%	68	32	100

Equal opportunity and time to all parties was found reasonable by a majority of elders. More members in the non-minister category supported this suggestion than the minister group. During interaction, ministers desired more time to ruling parties to explain their policies, programmes and developmental activities etc., to the voters since they held ministerial berths with the support of the electorate. Another point mentioned by them was that some parties in the State have failed to secure even 25% of the total seats (at times the strength is negligible) in spite of being on the political scene for quite a long time and said that equating all the parties is unjustified. Non-ministers' support in this regard is quite natural since the existing practice is advantageous to them.

Freedom of Expression

Before the commencement of party broadcasts a meeting of party representatives, media officials and Election Commissioner is held at national and regional levels to discuss the mode of party political campaigning over Radio and Television. The parties are advised to follow the code (framed by the Election Commission in consultation with the party representatives) while preparing the script. Accordingly the party representatives submit their scripts in advance to the media officials for scrutiny before the broadcast. Lot of criticism was aired in the past about this procedure. While some questioned the need for such a code since it curtails freedom of expression, others were sceptical about the competence of media officials in judging the scripts. But media authorities felt no need to deviate from the guidelines which were framed after taking many aspects into consideration. (In the Assembly elections (December, 1994) the scripts submitted by the political parties for AIR/T.V., broadcast were scrutinized by a committee of experts outside the official media). When the sample was approached for their opinions about these aspects more than half of the respondents (63.51%) stated that there is enough scope for freedom of expression in party broadcasts (Table No. 4.6). When analysed Party-wise, Congress (I) and Communists were satisfied with the guidelines (85.10% and 80% respectively), whereas TDP and BJP which were functioning as opposition parties (at the time of study) felt the opposite way (36% and 20% respectively) perhaps because of their active role in the opposition.

Agewise difference of opinion was seen in this regard. Whereas the younger politicians were equally divided over the freedom allowed, 57% of the middle aged group expressed satisfaction, but as many as 80.76% of the elders were happy with the freedom allowed. The progressive increase in the satisfaction along with the age (graph No. 4.1) reveals an obvious fact. Youngsters have a long political future and their concern for freedom of expression will be naturally more, whereas most of aged politicians are either retired from politics or not so active. For this sector, the effect of any change in the present level of freedom of expression in the media may be of little difference.

TABLE NO. 4.6 : **Distribution of responses whether enough freedom of expression is given in party broadcasts (Q. No. 6)**

Party		*Yes*	*No*	*Total*
Congress I	Fre	40	7	47
	%	85.10	14.89	-
T.D.P.	Fre	9	16	25
	%	36	64	-
B.J.P.	Fre	2	8	10
	%	20	80	-
Communist	Fre	8	2	10
	%	80	20	-
Others	Fre	2	2	4
	%	50	50	-
Total	Fre	61	35	96
	%	63.54	36.45	100

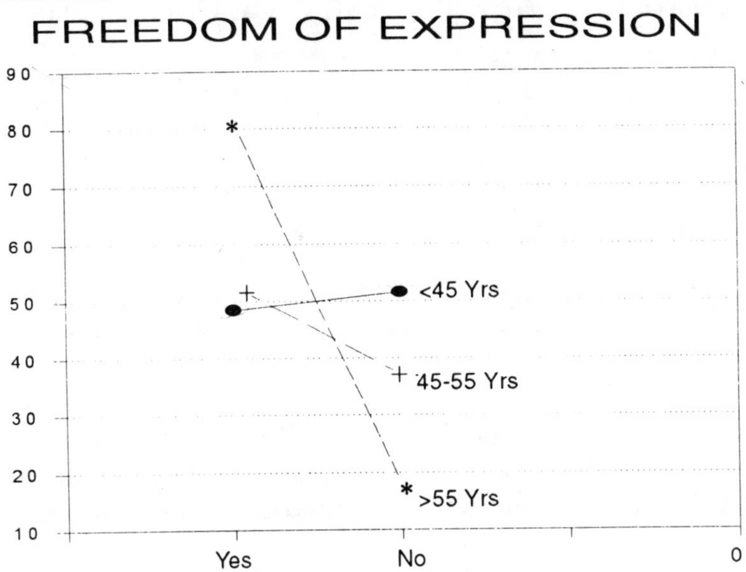

Graph No. 4.1

Election Code

Majority of the sample (92%) desired an election code for party broadcasts including Communist parties which were unanimous (Table No. 4.7). The other leaders who opposed suggested that the decision should be left to the people.

Generally, a wide range of public criticism is noticed in case of Radio/TV's role in respect of political matters because of the policies and restrictions imposed. It is, therefore, surprising to note that a majority of the political leaders who also usually criticize media's restrictions, desired election code for party broadcasts. The respondents' unanimity in their desire for maintaining orderliness and discipline in matters relating to political publicity is thus clear, though surprising.

TABLE NO. 4.7 : **Distribution of Responses on the Desirability of Election Code for Party Broadcasts (Q. No. 7).**

Party		*Yes*	*No*	*Total*
Congress (I)	Fre	46	4	50
	%	92	8	-
T.D.P.	Fre	22	3	25
	%	80	12	-
B.J.P.	Fre	9	1	10
	%	90	10	-
Communist	Fre	10	-	10
	%	100	-	-
Others	Fre	5	-	5
	%	100	-	-
Total	Fre & %	92	8	100

The sample was very specific that the code should be comprehensive so as to cover all the aspects including economic and other offences. The speaker must be penalised if the allegations made in the broadcasts are not substantiated. In fact, he/she may even be asked to submit an affidavit before naming such offences. On the question of formulation of code the respondents have varied ideas. A major group of respondents (73.91%) preferred All Party Committee, another group (14.13%) for Government i.e. Election Commission, and around 10% (mostly political thinkers) for a Public Committee consisting of intellectuals. (Table No. 4.8)

Even though the 10% (who opted for Public Committee) does not appear significant, the sample of this category constitutes mature and senior politicians and perhaps they could have thought that this Committee would truly reflect public opinion in these programmes. While one suggested the Committee may include high public figures like Chief Justice of Supreme Court or High Courts, others wanted the ex-presidents and educationists to find a place in the Committee.

TABLE NO. 4.8 : **Distribution of Preferences on who should form the Code (Q. No. 7a)**

Party		*Govt.*	*Media officials*	*All party committee*	*Public committee*	*Total*
Congress (I)	Fre	9	2	30	4	45
	%	20	4.44	66.66	8.88	-
T.D.P.	Fre	3	-	18	2	23
	%	13.04	-	78.26	8.69	-
B.J.P.	Fre	-	-	8	1	9
	%	-	-	88.88	11.11	-
Communist	Fre	1	-	7	2	10
	%	10	-	70	20	-
Others	Fre	-	-	5	-	5
	%	-	-	100	-	-
Total	Fre	13	2	68	9	92
	%	14.13	2.17	73.91	9.78	100

Editing the Script

With regard to the editing of the script by media officials a little more than half of the representatives

(56%) were positive in their approach (Table No. 4.9). Partywise there was no significant difference. Cong. (I) and Communists were in favour of the present practice whereas BJP did not show much inclination towards the existing procedure.

The politicians who often criticize Radio and TV for editing the scripts, have indeed given quite an unexpected response. There were instances where conflict cropped up due to the editing of the script by media authorities. The TDP once criticized Radio officials for editing their party broadcast script on the issue of Bofors and abstained from the broadcast. However interestingly 48% of TDP leaders consented for editing the script. But BJP's support of this aspect seems to be a bit less for reasons unknown.

TABLE NO. 4.9 : **Distribution of Responses on the need for editing the Script in Party Broadcasts (Q. No. 8)**

Party		*Necessary*	*Not necessary*	*Total*
Congress (I)	Fre	29	21	50
	%	58	42	-
T.D.P.	Fre	12	13	25
	%	48	52	-
B.J.P.	Fre	4	6	10
	%	40	60	-
Communist	Fre	8	2	10
	%	80	20	-
Others	Fre	3	2	5
	%	60	40	-
Total	Fre & %	56	44	100

The 44% who felt editing is not necessary were of the strong opinion that economic and political offences can be allowed to go in party broadcasts but acts of criminal conduct followed by slanderous personal allegations should be avoided to the maximum extent (Table No. 4.10). "Unless the first two offences are mentioned how can the voters assess the performance of a particular political party?", they asked.

TABLE NO. 4.10 : **Distribution of Responses on the Type of Offences that may be Allowed in Party Broadcast (Q. No. 8a)**

Party		*Economic Offences*			*Political Offences*			*Criminal Conduct*			*Slanderous personal allegations*		
		Yes	No	Total	Yes	No	Total	Yes	No	Total	Yes	No	Total
Cong.	Fre	17	4	21	18	3	21	15	6	21	6	15	21
	%	80.95	19.04	-	85.71	14.28	-	71.42	28.57	-	28.57	71.42	-
TDP	Fre	8	2	10	9	1	10	7	3	10	6	4	10
	%	80	20	-	90	10	-	70	30	-	60	40	-
BJP	Fre	6	1	7	6	1	7	3	4	7	1	6	7
	%	85.71	14.28	-	85.71	14.28	-	42.85	57.14	-	14.28	85.71	-
Comm-	Fre	4	-	4	4	-	4	4	-	4	-	4	4
unist	%	100	-	-	100	-	-	100	-	-	-	100	-
Others	Fre	1	1	2	1	1	2	1	1	2	-	2	2
	%	50	50	-	50	50	-	50	50	-	-	100	-
Total	Fre	36	8	44	38	6	44	30	14	44	13	31	44
	%	81.81	18.18	100	86.36	13.63	100	68.18	31.81	100	29.54	70.45	100

A minority group from Congress (I) and TDP who were against editing felt that even slanderous personal allegations could be permitted in the broadcasts. Personal discussions revealed two major reasons for such a view : (1) Public are sensible enough to judge arguments, and (2) Media authorities, show pronounced bias and favouritism while editing.

Agewise difference was also noticed in the responses to editing the script. While majority of the younger and elder party managers felt that the acts of criminal conduct can be allowed in party broadcasts in addition to political and economic offences, the middle age group is evenly divided and thus equally inclined to reject the idea as well. The active politicians (middle aged) might have perceived unwanted consequences in allowing the criminal offences and hence did not give full consent to the suggestion. While the junior party managers (first and second group) have shown considerable positive attitude in allowing slanderous personal allegations in the broadcast, seniors were unanimous in negating the idea. A positive response was branded as unthoughtful by many during personal discussions. However, the influence of age here reflects the maturity of elders. This discussion on the merits and demerits of the present system can be summed up with the following conclusions.

The leaders were quite content with the present system of broadcasts except in two aspects, the quantum and duration of the programmes. While full satisfaction was observed in case of 'timings of broadcasts and election code, Party-wise differences were observed in other areas i.e.' equal opportunity and time to both bigger and smaller parties and freedom of expression.

Editing the script by media officials was criticised by a significant group. Age and position of the sample have a bearing on the responses to some extent.

Chapter 5

MULTI-MEDIA CAMPAIGN

The distinctive feature of an election is that voters are subject to many influences simultaneously. The role of the opinion leader in influencing the voters was considered to be more important than of the mass media in the past, while recent research indicated a more direct contact between mass media and audience. Inter-personal relations are still considered as an effective medium by many especially in rural areas. However it was also observed that the sources of information for opinion leaders are definitely mass-media. The influence of these leaders is also observed to lessening as the individual's exposure to media is increasing and party loyalties are diminishing. A model of voting suggested by Rose and McAllister[1] gives a reasonable account of factors contributing to voting behaviour.

A Cumulative Lifetime Learning Model of Voting

PRE ADULT SOCIALIZATION			ADULT SOCIALIZATION EXPERIENCES
			POLITICAL PRINCIPLES
			PARTY PERFORMANCE IN PARLIAMENT
			ELECTION CAMPAIGN
			VOTE
(Birth)	(Age 18)	(Latest Parliament)	(Election day)

Landmark Dates In the life history of a voter

While mass media is very active during elections its role in other times also is not insignificant. Various components of mass media contribute to the cumulative political knowledge of the voters. The rapid growth of communication technology aided by satellites and computers is creating a new media world hitherto not experienced. Radio and Television are considered as the most effective and glamorous mass-media influencing the society. However the role of Broadcast media alone during elections cannot be discussed in isolation. Multi-media competition in election campaigns is increasing day by day. Agenda setting mechanism (discussed details also in Chapter No IX) could possibly explain the effectiveness of various media but, the major limitation in agenda setting theory is the difficulty in assessing each medium's contribution to the agenda set by a particular medium. The entire mechanism of election campaigning aims are shifting the opinion of the electorate. Hence, a political communication researcher cannot afford to ignore certain aspects especially the role of various media units in raising the political consciousness of the voters, nature of coverage and the strengths and weaknesses of each medium etc. What are the impressions of politicians about these media units in supporting their policies and programmes? A few questions pertaining to the role of different media units in party politics put to the sample and the responses are discussed below.

The Most Influential Medium

The sample was asked to give in order of preference their rating of the most influential media unit during elections. In response, Congress (I) and TDP gave first preference to door-to-door campaign as they felt that it was the most influential medium (Table No. 5.1). The second preference was Press for Congress and Public meetings for TDP. In contrast, BJP considered TV followed by Press and Communist leaders preferred Press followed by Radio as the most effective media.

TABLE NO. 5.1 : **Distribution of Responses on the most Influencing Media Unit (Q. No. 1)**

Party		*Press*	*Films*	*Tele-visi-on*	*Wall Posters/ Pamphlets/ leaflets*	*Door to door campaign*	*Public meetings*	*Radio*	*Audio and video cassettes*
Congress (I)	% responded	74	26	56	26	62	56	50	28
	mean score	2	4.53	2.6	3.5	1.87	3	3.2	4
T.D.P.	% responded	92	24	64	48	64	72	44	32
	mean score	2.39	4.5	3.56	3.83	2.12	2.33	3.45	3.62
B.J.P.	% responded	90	60	80	40	80	70	40	40
	mean score	2.77	4.66	1.37	6.5	3.5	5	3.5	3.25
Communist	% responded	80	20	60	60	70	70	50	10
	mean score	1.62	5	3.83	4.5	3.57	3.4	2.2	5
Others	% responded	100	-	40	-	80	80	20	20
	mean score	2.2	-	2.5	-	2.25	2.5	1	3

During personal discussions, the leaders expressed that door-to-door campaign, though most effective, is humanly impossible as it needed coverage of huge population and area. Advantage of direct contact apart, election campaign through public meetings has its limitations too. While accepting the potentiality of Broadcast media in influencing the voters, the politicians must have selected Press as the first choice in view of its long established active role in politics.

Radio and TV, however, effective they may be, were not preferred by many of the respondents, apparently because of their silence over conflictive and controversial issues in politics. Some were even of the opinion that Radio and TV cannot claim any influence on voting behaviour and equate themselves with the Press.

The sample of above 55 age rated the Press one point higher as the most influential medium, while TV found favour with the youngsters. On the other hand, ministers gave a little higher score to public meetings than the non-ministers.

Radio and TV as Campaign Tools

It is a known fact that the leaders are not solely dependent on party broadcasts. It can also be said that they concentrate and depend more on other modes of campaigning than on Radio and TV. Then why so much competition, interest and criticism among them for these programmes? To a question as to what made them agree give party broadcasts over Radio and TV, most of the politicians highlighted the potentiality of the Broadcast media in reaching large masses in short time and claimed Broadcast media as more effective compared to other media of mass-communication. (Table No 5.2). Reasons like "because the facility is available", "attraction towards the glamour of the media" "because other parties are availing the facility" and "no financial implications" etc. were also mentioned by the sample.

While accepting the potential of the media as the prime reason for participating in party broadcasts, the sample giving some cognisable score to the option "because the facility is available" reflects a passive attitude and creates an impression that the absence of such facility also would not matter much to them. This appears to be an aspect where media people have to give some thought.

Agewise, elders, and positionwise, ministers subscribed to this aspect slightly more than others. This response reflects an indifference of the representatives for using the broadcasts coupled with an element of practical thinking. However, this may not call for serious thought since these reasons were given last preference by a majority of the sample including younger politicians and ministers. Among the reasons quoted by the sample for supporting party broadcasts two distinct features were observed.

1. It is a universal phenomenon that media are utilised for publicity purposes, and
2. Democracy has come to stay and the people have a right/need to get more acquainted with this type of information and propaganda for decision making.

Film Stars as Vote Grabbers

Films have been acclaimed as the most effective audiovisual media. In spite of the advantages of Television, films have not lost their popularity. On the other hand, most of the film based programmes on T.V. are observed to be very popular. Film stars entering into the political arena have drawn the attention of the voters and gained much prominence

TABLE NO. 5.2 : **Distribution of Preferences for Party Broadcasts (Q. No. 9)**

Party		*Broadcast media is more effective compared to other media of mass communications*	*Because the facility is available*	*To reach more in less time*	*Glamour of the media attracts me*	*Because other parties are availing the facility*	*No financial implications*	*Others*
Congress (I)	% responded	70	22	92	20	14	66	12
	Mean score	1.85	2.90	1.45	3.1	4.28	2.63	2.66
T.D.P.	% responded	84	44	92	28	16	64	-
	Mean score	2	2.90	1.39	3.42	4.00	3.06	-
B.J.P.	% responded	80	30	90	20	10	20	-
	Mean score	1.37	4	1.55	4.00	6.00	2.5	-
Communist	% responded	60	40	80	-	20	40	10
	Mean score	1.66	1.75	1.37	-	3.00	3.5	4.00
Others	% responded	80	40	100	40	-	20	-
	Mean score	1.25	2	1.8	3	-	3	-

in political circles. It is also observed that film personalities are grabbing more votes even without political experience. In response to a question put to the sample (including some film stars-turned-politicians) to know the main reason for film personalities winning elections, Cong. (I), TDP and Communist parties felt hero-worship promoted by the media and glamorous image as the major considerations (Table No. 5.3). While supporting the hero-worship thesis, BJP added that their interest in politics also counted to a great extent, as popularity alone cannot make a politician.

During discussion, it was observed that the leaders are not happy since many mature and senior politicians were rejected party tickets in preference to film personalities and the seriousness of politics is spoilt by cinema gimmicks. The reason why the film personalities do not contest as independents is that their success owes to party base and not to glamour alone, they argue. In reaction, the film personalities posed the question : what is wrong if film stars desire to serve the people through politics?

It is interesting to note that the present general election (during which the study was conducted) has more or less exploded the myth that film stars could grab more votes, since many of the star turned politicians, especially in Andhra Pradesh, lost the contest. However recognition of hero-worship as the chosen factor for the film actors' success in election indirectly hints that leadership quality whether acquired or created is an important characteristic for any politician. Masses desire to be led by some one, preferably by a charismatic personality. It can be further said that media can upbring a politician mainly at two stages, by familiarising at first level and by publicizing at the second; with its status conferral role, it definitely helps people in politics a great deal.

TABLE NO. 5.3 : **Distribution of Reasons for Film Personalities Winning More Voters (Q. No. 13).**

Party		*Extensive media exposure*	*Political image created by the medium*	*Their genuine activities & concern for the masses*	*Hero-worship promoted by the medium*	*Glamorous image*	*Their political awarness/ maturity*
Congress (I)	% responded	60	28	10	88	82	18
	Mean score	2.46	3.21	3.8	1.63	1.70	3.77
T.D.P.	% responded	60	24	12	52	80	16
	Mean score	2.2	3.33	3	1.92	1.5	4.75
B.J.P.	% responded	50	20	20	70	60	10
	Mean score	1.8	4	1	1.85	2.16	1
Communist	% responded	60	20	20	50	70	20
	Mean score	2	3	3	2.6	1.57	4
Others	% responded	40	20	-	100	100	40
	Mean score	2	1	-	2	1.6	3

More number of elders claimed that political awareness and service concern for the masses, apart from glamour and hero-worship created by the silver screen, are the reasons for the film stars' success in elections.

According to one politician, film personalities winning elections is not because of glamour or any such thing but due to the political wave prevailing at the time of elections. Another opinion is that a film actor's character, oratory and the type of roles they play in the films also make some difference.

Audio Video Cassettes

Critics think that the passivity experienced over long years and the desire to have a say in the media programmes has led the people to opt for two-way communication system. The new technology has solved the problem of one-way communication through two-way cable and interactive television. But this is not yet widespread in the Indian context and is still in infancy. However, one can observe the rapid growth of narrow casting technology in our society. As the term denotes, this is antonym to broadcasting. The limitations of broadcasting have given rise to the demassification of the media i.e. narrow casting. Audio and video cassettes, cable TV etc. fall under this category. One of the limitations of Radio and T.V. as observed by media critics is while catering to the interests of millions, they are not able to satisfy specialized groups. In spite of many analytical programmes, magazine programmes etc. these clusters of audience are not fully satisfied. The video revolution which initially began to serve entertainment purposes slowly creeped into specialized areas. Due to many advantages they could become the potential media. Their use in political affairs needs no emphasis again.

The lone limitation of these media in a developing country is their high cost. But the present trend shows that even this factor does not matter much to the people.

In the recent elections audio video cassettes played a significant role as campaign media. But why are politicians depending on these expensive devices? What are the advantages of this popular technology? The respondents unanimously claimed audio and video cassettes as the most effective means of election campaign (Table No 5.4). In addition to the non-availability of enough publicity, time and scope over Radio and TV, there are many other factors to be taken into consideration in deciding the popularity and effectiveness of this mode of publicity. Freedom of expression, scope for mobility, adaptability to local needs, facility to incorporate required changes, immediacy etc. are claimed to be some of the reasons for its preferene. It is observed that even if sufficient time is provided over Radio and TV, audio and video cassettes may have their own place in electronic campaigning. When small media like A.V. Cassettes without any broadcasting facility can play an important role in the present day elections, one can imagine the scope of radio and television as campaign tools if proper interest, imagination and innovation are applied. It is surprising to note that the politicians are concentrating highly on preparing programmes on audio and video cassettes without bothering much for Radio/TV. This also makes one think whether Radio/TV can face the stiff competition from A.V. cassettes in future, even if they improve the quality of the production. However according to some individual opinions, these cassettes are no alternative to Broadcast media and serve only entertainment purposes. This is not a healthy trend and makes politics a cheap amusement affair. One politician claimed that AV cassettes are trying to exploit religious fundamentalism.

TABLE NO. 5.4 : **Distribution of Responses on the use of Audio and Video Cassettes during Elections. (Q.No. 14)**

Party		*They are more effective means to reach the voters.*	*Broadcast media is not giving enough publicity/time/scope*	*They can be repeated as many times as required*	*Freedom of expression of political view.*
Congress (I)	% responded	84	52	88	74
	Mean score	1.38	2.53	2.15	2.43
T.D.P.	% responded	88	56	86	72
	Mean score	1.59	2.42	2.37	2.33
B.J.P.	% responded	90	50	70	60
	Mean score	1.55	2.2	2.42	1.83
Communist	% responded	80	20	70	50
	Mean score	1.37	2.5	2	2.8
Others	% responded	100	-	100	60
	Mean score	1	-	2.2	2.3

Local Radios in Politics

Local radio stations are a recent development in Indian Broadcasting. As the term denotes, the programmes are need-oriented. A question was put to seek the views of the sample about the role of the local radios in future politics. As Table No. 5.5 shows, a bulk of the sample (82%) responded positively. 59.49% see a major role for the local the radios whereas 39.24% visualised only a minor role (Table No. 5.6).

Congress (I) and BJP who did not give any score to Radio in future politics (Table no 5.7) have however endorsed the possible active role of local radios in future politics (78% and 90% respectively). TDP the only party which attached some importance to Radio naturally responded positively (84%) and Communists who offered negligible values to the effectiveness of

Radio have also responded enthusiastically with a high percentage (90%). About the extent of the role, Congress(I) and TDP are more optimistic of Radio playing a major role, whereas BJP expressed less hopes and communists weighed both equally. These opinions do reflect a role for local radio, whether minor or major.

TABLE NO. 5.5 : **Distribution of Responses on the Role of Local Radios in Future Politics (Q. No. 38)**

Party		*Yes*	*No*	*Total*
Congress - (I)	Fre.	39	11	50
	%	78	22	—
T.D.P.	Fre.	21	4	25
	%	84	16	—
B.J.P.	Fre.	9	1	10
	%	90	10	—
Communist	Fre.	9	1	10
	%	90	10	—
Others	Fre.	4	1	5
	%	80	20	—
Total	Fre. & %	82	18	100

TABLE NO. 5.6 : **Distribution of Responses on the extent of Local Radios Role in Future Politics (Q. No. 38a)**

Party		*Major*	*Minor*	*Nil*	*Don't know*	*Total*
Congress (I)	Fre.	25	14	—	—	39
	%	64.10	35.89	—	—	—
T.D.P.	Fre.	11	8	—	1	20
	%	55	40	—	5.1	—
B.J.P.	Fre.	4	5	—	—	9
	%	44.44	55.55	—	—	—
Communist	Fre.	4	4	—	—	8
	%	50	50	—	—	—
Others	Fre.	3	—	—	—	3
	%	100	—	—	—	—
Total	Fre.	47	31	—	1	79
	%	59.49	39.24	—	1.26	—

While middle aged and senior politicians expressed hopes about local radios playing an active role in future politics, youngsters were less optimistic in this regard. However, the first-two groups found the extent of role to be major. Contrary to this, the elders see a minor role here. Juniors' disinterest in local radios is understandable from the earlier discussions but their answers to the supplementary question (extent of role) can be interpreted as below. Basically they are sceptical about the role of local radios in future politics keeping in view the present mode of functioning of the medium. But if Radio takes some interest in future, the effect could be certainly good. Elders who were positive about local radio's role in future politics have not considered the role to be a major one, may be because they do not want to build high hopes over theoretical foundations.

According to some individual opinions local radios can be of much help to politicians if they are independent. Door-to-door campaign which is an effective mode can be well replaced by local radios. Though the sample could not perceive immediately the type of political programming on local radios, they were positive about the strength of this medium in political matters. The leaders, who gave very little score to Radios in the previous responses, also were optimistic about local radios. What could be the reason for this contradiction? Apparently, the demographical factors!

The rural voters who constitutes a high percentage of population are more important for the politicians. TV, in addition to other limitations, suffers from urbanness. In spite of Government's stress on developmental programmes, rural participation and mass education, Broadcast media is finding it difficult to achieve its objectives due to the pressure from urban audience. The concept of local radio was introduced to ward off these difficulties. The sample must have thought that to reach the rural voters, local radio is the best means, since TV is yet to make its impact due to aforesaid limitations. However, the fulfilment of these hopes largely depends on the nature of political programmes that would be transmitted from local radios.

Suitable Media for Politics in Future

To a question which medium in their opinion will be more helpful to persons who aspire for a political career in future, as many as 47.9 per cent preferred newspapers followed by TV (38.54%) and the other responses were negligible. (Table No. 5.7)

TABLE NO. 5.7 : **Distribution of Responses on the Choice of Medium for Promoting Future Political Career (Q. No. 37)**

Party		*Films*	*Television*	*Radio*	*News-papes*	*Others*	*Total*
Congress (I)	Fre.	4	22	—	20	2	48
	%	8.33	45.83	—	41.66	4.16	—
T.D.P.	Fre.	—	8	2	13	1	24
	%	—	33.33	8.33	54.16	4.16	—
B.J.P.	Fre.	—	5	—	5	—	10
	%	—	50	—	50	—	—
Communist	Fre.	1	1	1	6	—	
	%				66.66	—	—
Others	Fre.	1	1	1	2	—	5
	%	20	20	20	40	—	—
Total	Fre.	6	37	4	46	3	96
	%	6.25	38.54	4.16	47.91	3.12	—

Communists preferred newspapers and gave negligible score to other media. BJP categorically favoured newspapers and TV equally (50% each) and almost equal interest was shown by TDP and Congress (I) in newspapers and TV. Here TDP attach some importance to Radio also (8.33%). Some suggested that all media units can be employed together towards this goal. It was also felt that selection of a medium depends on certain aspects like mode of propaganda, financial resources of the particular party etc. More familiarity with conventional media could be the reason for communists' skewed response in this regard.

TV was rated second in order of preference. Here also elders gave less score compared to others. They would not have found TV an active medium in politics during the past decades nor even now, and may not have great hopes for future also, whereas the middle aged and younger groups expressed optimism for the future. Position-wise ministers pinned much hopes on TV and non-ministers on newspapers. The latter group also attached some importance to Radio (6.45%) whereas ministers did not see any hope in Radio.

While the preference for Press and Television is understandable, Radio scoring very low may need further analysis. Radio has enjoyed high level popularity for more than three decades. In spite of TV's domination radio still has its popularity intact in many countries. As such the low score in a pointer directs Radio to restructure and redesign its programmes taking into cognizance the prevailing heavy competition. The reason for the sample not being inclined towards Radio in future politics could be that Radio for many decades gained popularity mostly for its "news" programme. It is generally felt that Radio gives only information but no analysis or views of such information. Even though Press was more active, radio could play a vital role all these years mainly due to its access to common man and appeal to illiterates carrying along various criticisms. Even though T.V. puts no additional efforts in the presentation of political affairs compared to Radio, it could extend some opportunity to the politicians due to newness, glamour and visual impact (where events become reality on the screen). Is Radio, therefore, really going to have a small role in future politics? This is a point which needs serious thinking by the policy makers.

Radio is immediate, cost effective and pervasive; the major drawback for TV being the non-availability of sets in rural areas. But the plus points of Radio have no value in the absence of effective programming. One of the factors responsible for TV's domination over Radio seems to be the latter's inertia in coping with the demanding situation. Each medium differs from the other in nature and there are some similarities too. Each has its own advantages and disadvantages. As Tyrrel[2] observes, a newspaper man can gather news most quickly, but hours must elapse before it is ready for public. A television team may take hours to shoot and get the film back to the studios but transmission to the viewer is instantaneous. A newspaper man can spend an hour interviewing a man, and condense the material into one or two minutes reading time. The television reporter must extract the essence on the spot. What he gets on film can be cut, not condensed. Speaking about Radio, Barwise and Ehrenberg[3] say, Radio is more like Television than the other media but there are also marked differences. Radio, like poetry, can picture events in the mind's eye or concentrate on meaning and sound. It can similarly defy space, time and nature. This freedom can on occasion make Radio listening a memorably powerful experience. However, it requires exceptional writing and performance, and considerable effort from the listener.

Based on production factors and consumption factors there are many similarities and differences among these media units. Normally, one would expect each medium to reflect its individual characteristics in reporting elections. For example, Radio is characterised by immediacy, TV by visual support and Press by the additional details etc. But, as many observe neither in content nor in technique all these media could make their mark in reporting vividly. Criticizing the media reporting of election news as "Pack journalism", Gamble and Gamble[4] say, "most reporters following a campaign cover it in pretty much the same way. Journalists on the campaign trail with a candidate usually stay in the same hotels, ride the same buses and planes, attend the same press conferences, and interview the same aides to the candidates. By spending so much time with one another, and by hearing and reading the same material, it is not surprising that they come to similar conclusions. When they break away from the "Pack" and adopt novel interpretations of campaign, their editors tend to doubt them and are reluctant to publish or broadcast the different views. This especially true when the independent reporter is fairly new on the job.

While broadcasting serves the needs of huge masses narrowcasting caters to the demands of specific groups. The disadvantage of one medium becomes the advantage of the other. The new media (A.V. Cassette, cable TV etc.) has emerged as an alternative in communication and the increasing choosiness of voters has forced the contenders to consider the strengths and weaknesses of each medium.

However, with the help of the available hardware facilities, Radio and TV can devise "talkback systems" (already in practice) and use them extensively to solve the problem of passivity among the audience. For example, formats like Live audience programmes, panel programmes and phone-ins may give scope for more audience participation. When each medium realizes how distinctly it can report party politics depending on the merits and demerits inherent in it, mass media can extend a meaningful support to the body politic in democracy.

The following are thus the major conclusions on the roles of different media.

The leaders have not categorically mentioned any medium to be superior to the other but critically weighed the strengths and weak points of each system. The main basis for their judgement seems to be the role played by each medium in the present political context. While claiming broadcast media as highly potential they were unanimous in appreciating the role of audio and video cassettes and films in election exercises.

Though Radio was not declared as a potent political medium by a majority, the politicians pinned great hopes on local radios in future politics in view of their easy access to rural voters.

Door-to-door campaign followed by press and television were rated as the most influential media during elections by majority of the leaders though they differed partywise. Newspapers followed by Television were accorded greater role in future politics with slight partywise differences.

Age and position exhibited considerable influence on the responses.

REFERENCES

1. Rose, Richard and McAllister, Ian: Voters begin to choose- From closed class to open elections in Britain; London, Sage Publications, 1986, p. 127.
2. Tyrrel, Robert; *The Work of the Television Journalist*; London. Focal Press 1972, p. 10.
3. Barwise, Patrick and Ehrenbergh, Andrew; *Television and its Audience*; London, Sage Publications Ltd., 1988, p. 130.
4. Gamble, Michael W. and Gamble, Teri Kwal; *Introducing Mass Communications*; Singapore, McGraw Hill Book Co., 1989, p. 402.

Chapter 6

CONCEPTIONS ABOUT THE AUDIENCE

Knowledge of the target audience, a prerequisite for any broadcast, helps the producer as well as the presenter in bringing out effective and lively programmes. This applies to party broadcasts too. The leaders are expected to have enough knowledge of their audience for whom their speeches are meant. This needs collection of information from available research or through the assistance of special agencies involved. But politicians rarely seek such sources. We are, therefore, left to wonder: What are their conceptions about the audience? To what extent they care to think about the media habits and nature of the audience while preparing their party Broadcasts? The second part of the questionnaire concentrated on these aspects.

Types of Audience : Rural—Urban

While urban masses are directly exposed to media, interpersonal communication channels play an important role in rural areas. A well known example is the use of folk forms for communicating messages to rural masses. This may raise a doubt whether the rural folk who constitute a major part of our population are really able to appreciate media compaigning. However, as many as 80% of the sample felt that rural masses were moderately knowledgeable to appreciate the Broadcast media-campaigning (Table No.6.1), while 14% (mostly TDP) expressed that they were highly knowledgeable, BJP and Communist leaders viewed their knowledge as moderate. It may be observed that generally politicians are in constant touch with the rural folk in their constituencies and also during campaigning. The TDP gave 25% support to masses being "highly knowledgeable". Three reasons can be advanced in support of this argument. (1) The founder leader of TDP is an actor turned politician and very much popular among rural masses as a screen God. (2) Till recently the younger generation in Andhra Pradesh especially rural youth evinced more interest towards TDP. (3) The TDP was very popular among rural folk for its Rs. 2 per kg. rice scheme. (It may be stated that at present T.D.P. regained power in A.P. and according to political thinkers the pre-election promise of Rs 2 per kg. rice scheme mostly helped the party in winning the election).

TABLE NO. 6.1 : **Distribution of Responses on the Knowledgeability of Rural Folk in Appreciating the Media Campaign (Q. No. 17)**

Party		*Highly Knowledge-able*	*Moderately Knowledge-able*	*Not Knowle-dgeable*	*Cannot Say*	*Total*
Congress (I)	Fre.	7	41	1	1	50
	%	14	82	2	2	—
T.D.P.	Fre.	7	15	1	2	25
	%	28	60	4	8	—
B.J.P.	Fre.	—	10	—	—	10
	%	—	100	—	—	—
Communist	Fre.	—	10	—	—	10
	%	—	100	—	—	—
Others	Fre.	—	4	1	—	5
	%	—	80	20	—	—
Total	Fre&%.	14	80	3	3	100

Heavy Viewers/Medium Viewers

Based on the level of exposure to Radio/TV. (in terms of time of spent, involvement and preference of programmes etc.) the audience are generally categorised as heavy viewers/listeners (who regularly use T.V./Radio), medium viewers/ listeners (moderate use) and light viewers/listeners (occasional exposure). There is a notion that more exposure to media will have greater impact and may bring about desired changes in attitudes in the long run. The respondents seemed to support this as they felt that heavy viewers followed by medium viewers are likely to be more influenced by party broadcasts (Table No. 6.2)

TABLE NO. 6.2 : **Distribution of Responses on the Impact of Intensity of Viewing of Party Broadcasts by the Audience (Q. No. 18)**

Party		*Heavy viewers/ listeners*	*Medium viewers/ listeners*	*Light viewers/ listeners*
Congress (I)	% responded	56	60	46
	Mean score	1.42	1.6	2.47
T.D.P.	% responded	72	72	44
	Mean score	1.44	1.61	2.45
B.J.P.	% responded	60	70	40
	Mean score	1.33	1.42	2.75
Communist	% responded	60	40	10
	Mean score	1.16	1.25	3
Others	% responded	80	100	80
	Mean score	2.5	1.6	1.75

Committed/Non-committed Voters

Most of the studies on political communication research centred around elections and the thrust was to know the exact turnout of voters after listening to or watching party broadcasts. The main concern was to know the types of audience showing interest in party broadcasts since election aims at shift in opinion through persuasion. Studies revealed that the target group for media campaign are generally 'neutral voters'.

But who are these neutral voters? Rose and McAllister[1] give a detailed description about the characteristics of these wobblers and floaters during elections.

> "In open electoral competition a large fraction of voters are predisposed to wobble in their committment to a party and some will float between parties. When voting is indeterminate individuals do not need to change their class or socio-economic interests in order to change parties; all parties seek votes on a cross-class basis, appealing to many socio-economic interests. Nor do individuals need to change their principles, inasmuch as parties tend to accommodate many different views in order to recruit support from a cross-section of the electorate. In an open electorate, the distance between parties is less and far more easily traversed than in a closed electorate where there are social and ideological gulfs between parties. The openness of the electorate is best measured in a series of steps and half-steps. Stable voters do not change their behaviour from one election to the next, or at least, do not report acting differently between elections. Mobile voters are of three types :(1) those who move in-and-out of the ranks of being non-voters whether beause of coming of age or dying or temporarily being non-voters, (2) floating voters who have moved between parties in the recent past, and (3) wobbling voters, who are unsure of whether to vote the same or float to another party. In an open electorate, a majority of the electors will be mobile, and stable voters a minority. There is only one way for a voter to be stable, acting as before, but there are many possible directions in which a mobile voter can move."

But the representatives' opinion in the present study is apparently different probably because of the options given especially of the category 'voters with general interest in politics'. According to a majority of the sample (55%) the above category show more enthusiasm in party broadcasts. A group (26%) preferred committed voters and the rest (19%) non-committed voters (Table No. 6.3).

TABLE NO. 6.3 : **Distribution of Responses on the Type of Audience showing more Interest in Party Broadcasts (Q. No. 19)**

Party		*Commit-ted voters*	*Non commit-ted voters*	*Voters with general interest in politics*	*Don't know*	*Total*
Congress (I)	Fre	14	6	29	—	49
	%	28.57	12.24	59.18	—	—
T.D.P.	Fre	3	4	18	—	25
	%	12	16	72	—	—
B.J.P.	Fre	3	7	—	—	10
	%	30	70	—	—	—
Communist	Fre	4	1	5	—	10
	%	40	10	50	—	—
Others	Fre	2	—	3	—	5
	%	40	—	60	—	—
Total	Fre	26	18	55	—	99
	%	26.26	18.18	55.55	—	100

In the Indian context party broadcasts are treated more or less on par with any other programme. Hence these broadcasts could not influence the decision making power of voters.[2] This may perhaps be the reason for the category 'non-committed voters' scoring low as compared to committed voters who usually are interested in knowing the performance of their candidate over the media. Comparisons across the parties revealed that BJP ranked 'non-committed voters' first (70%) followed by 'committed (30%). Communists opted for 'committed voters' (40%) signifying their ideology. While majority selected voters with general interest in politics, BJP did not subscribe to this at all. Instead, 70% of them thought of the "non-committed voters" and only 30% opined that "committed voters" show more enthusiasm in these programmes. One would normally have expected BJP to depend more on "committed voters" given their strong accent on party ideology and cadre. It seems that they are of the idea that party broadcasts are mainly aimed at non-committed voters. However, this supports the views of the earlier researchers in this area. It is pertinent to quote Blumler[3] who analysed the dependency of undecided voters on Television medium in his "Media effects research".

> "It is the large group of political unsophisticates who are most likely to be susceptible to having the electoral context prescribed for them by TV. They have no alternative sources of information readily at hand since they are only casually interested in politics, and lack of motivation to seek out differing views on political issues. Yet, spurred on by public affairs programming and a vague sense that it is their duty to vote, they enter the electoral fray and fulfil the obligations as bequeathed by TV. It is among these unsophisticates that the influence of TV is likely to be substantial and in turn, the effect of the unsophisticates on the larger electoral process may be consequential. The political system may become even more volatile as increasingly large number of citizens are mobilized to participate through the medium of TV with unsophisticates floating in and out of the electorate. Newly enfranchised citizens moreover may see little utility in identifying with a political party as the functions performed by the party organisation continue to atrophy the political system and as TV increases its influence in providing frames of reference for elections, defining issues and candidates, organising cognitions specifying different postures

on issues and evaluating the performance of candidates through a variety of public affairs programmes".

Men vs. Women Audience

Sex is an important variable in impact assessment. Even though women have equal opportunity to be exposed to media programmes as men, they do not seem to show much interest in politics. Hence, there is a need to know which kind of men and women show interest in party broadcasts. The sample opined that among men, intellectuals (47.6%) followed by labour (29.06%) and employees (16.60%) pay more attention to party broadcasts (Table No. 6.4) Among women, housewives outnumbered (46.59%) both working women and youth 23.86% each (Table No. 6.5). It was observed that the sample were not enthusiastic of this categorisation of the audience though they agreed such knowledge about the target group could be beneficial for preparing a party broadcast.

TABLE NO. 6.4 : **Distribution of Responses on Men of Different Categories affected by the Party Broadcasts (Q. No. 20)**

Party		*Intellectuals*	*Businessmen*	*Employees*	*Labour*	*Total*
Congress (I)	Fre	17	2	12	11	42
	%	40.47	4.76	28.57	26.19	—
T.D.P.	Fre	10	—	3	10	23
	%	43.47	—	13.04	43.47	—
B.J.P.	Fre	6	1	1	1	9
	%	66.66	11.11	11.11	11.11	—
Communist	Fre	6	—	—	1	7
	%	85.71	—	—	14.28	—
Others	Fre	2	1	—	2	5
	%	40	20	—	40	—
Total	Fre	41	4	16	25	86
	%	47.67	4.65	18.60	29.06	100

Rural-Urban Difference

Urban-rural difference is a marked feature in India. One can see a vast difference between the 'urban' who are usually educated and the 'rural' who are mostly illiterate mass. Broadcast media in India is striving to cater to the varied needs of this composition of people with limited channels. To a question as to whose response they perceived as positive to party broadcasts majority (57%) of the leaders expressed confidence in rural masses but those who put faith in the urban voters is also not negligible (39%) (Table No. 6.5). This response can be considered to be significant since urban viewers are generally thought to be critical and non-dependable and the rural masses gullible.

TABLE NO. 6.5 : **Distribution of Responses on Women of Different Categories Showing Interest in Party Broadcasts (Q. No. 20a)**

Party		*House Wife*	*Working Women*	*Youth*	*Labour*	*Total*
Congress I	Fre	20	9	12	2	43
	%	46.51	20.93	27.90	4.65	—
T.D.P.	Fre	9	6	5	3	23
	%	39.13	26.08	21.73	13.04	—
B. J.P.	Fre	5	2	3	—	10
	%	50	20	30	—	—
Communist	Fre	6	1	—	—	7
	%	85.71	14.28	—	—	—
Other	Fre	1	3	1	—	5
	%	20	60	20	—	—
Total	Fre	41	21	21	5	88
	%	46.59	23.86	23.86	5.68	100

Partywise analysis showed (Table No. 6.6) that Cong.(I) and TDP expressed similar views as above, whereas BJP gave equal score (50%) to both rural and urban voters. While Communists attached more score to urban masses (55.55%), others (4.12%) could not decide. BJP and Communist parties have more sympathisers in urban areas. Especially the Communist parties consists of many educated youth though their cause is for the common man. The communist party has different ideology, arising out of its alien origins and global presence. Even though it has followers in rural areas, its appreciation and understanding is apparently more among intellectuals and, therefore, more in urban areas. BJP which is more popular in urban areas is slowly attracting the rural youth also. These could be the reasons for the two parties deviating slightly from the general opinion.

TABLE NO. 6.6 : **Distribution of Responses as per Rural-Urban Background of Voters Respond more Positively to Political Messages (Q. No. 21)**

Party		*Rural masses*	*Urban masses*	*Don't know*	*Total*
Congress (I)	Fre.	26	19	3	48
	%	54.16	39.58	6.25	—
T.D.P.	Fre.	17	8	—	25
	%	68	32	—	—
B.J.P.	Fre.	5	5	—	10
	%	50	50	—	—
Communist	Fre.	3	5	1	9
	%	33.33	55.55	11.11	—
Others	Fre.	4	1	—	5
	%	80	20	—	—
Total	Fre.	55	38	4	97
	%	56.70	39.17	4.12	—

Influence of Age and Position on the Responses

Influence of age is quite significant in this part. The seniors are clear than the other two groups about the type of audience that show more interest in Party Broadcasts (Graph No. 6.1 to 6.5). Eventhough all agreed that rural masses are moderately knowledgeable to appreciate the Broadcast media campaigning, the elders outnumbered others in

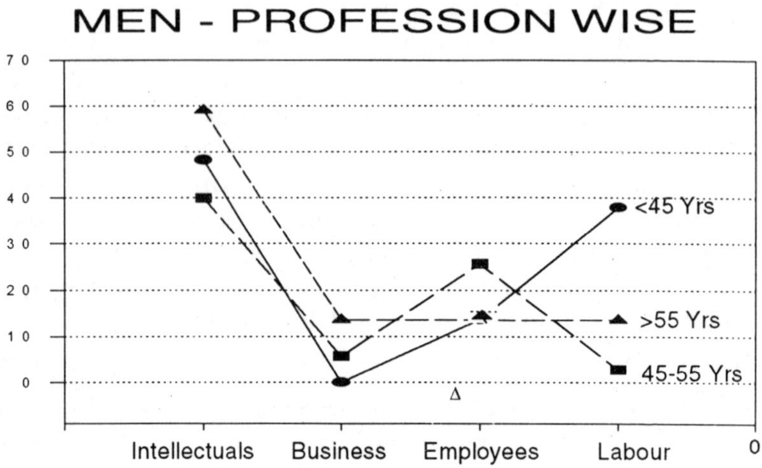

Graph No. 6.1

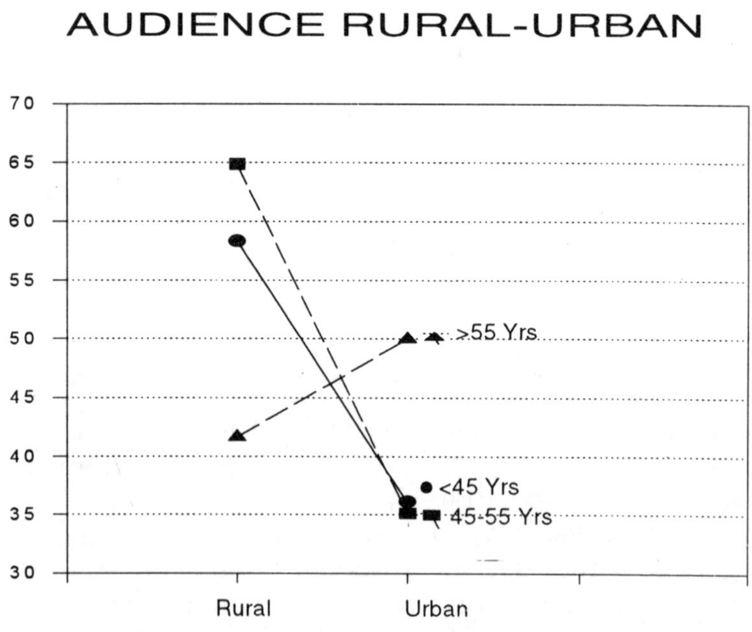

Graph No. 6.2

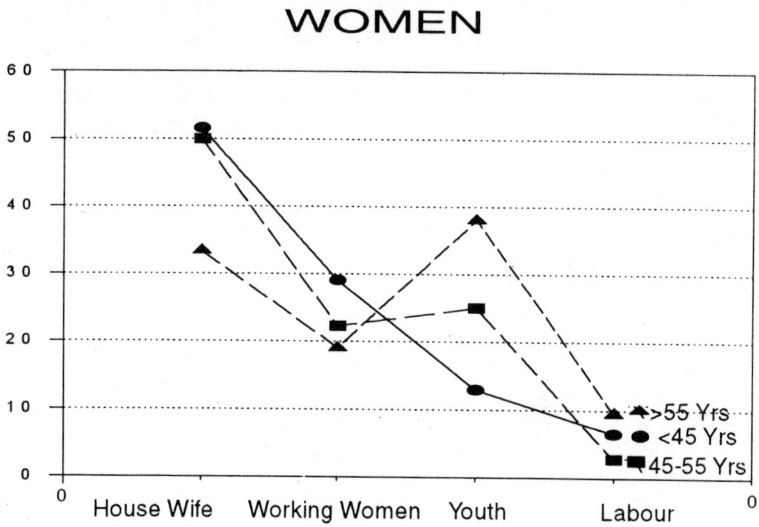

Graph No. 6.3

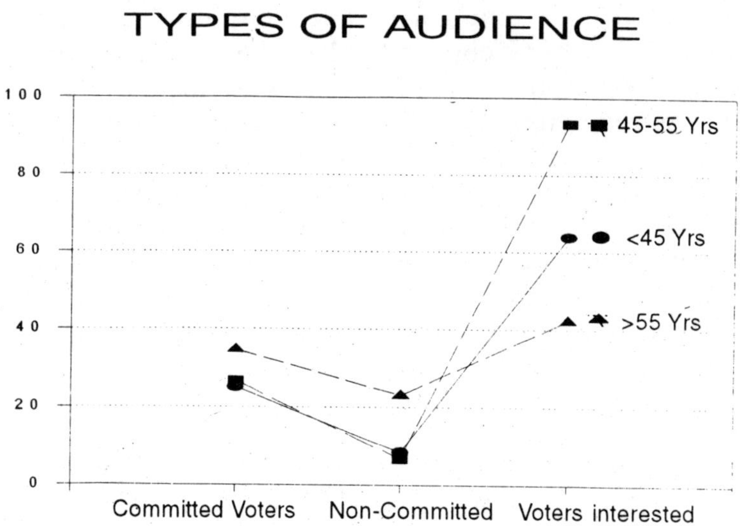

Graph No. 6.4

KNOWLEDGE OF RURAL FOLK IN APPRECIATING MEDIA CAMPAIGNING

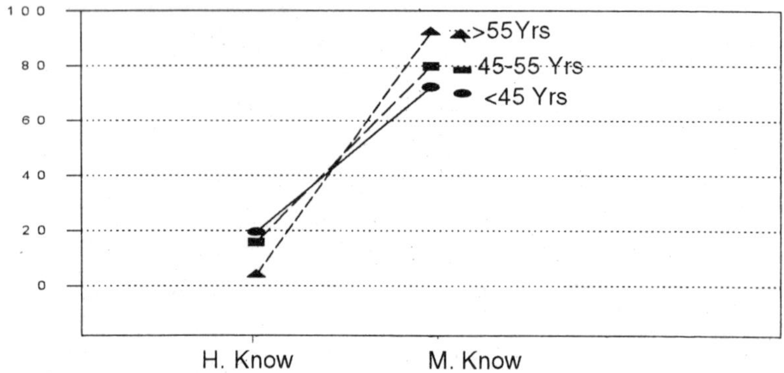

Graph No. 6.5

expressing more faith. While the voters with general interest in politics scored high in the response, they also rated other categories i.e. committed and non-committed voters considerably. Another area where agewise difference in responses was observed to be quite significant is the influence of PBs among different categories of men. The youngest group broadly gave equal preference to intellectuals and labour followed by others. The next age group (between 45-55) rated intellectuals more followed by labour and employees. It is noteworthy that elders gave 50% score to intellectuals and attached low importance to others. However in this group 'no response' category constitutes 19%. In addition to the samples' conception about the type of audience this also reflects their general opinion about PBs that party campaigning over Radio and TV is well received and understood mostly by intellectuals.

In case of women's response to PB's also a similar viewpoint was noticed. The young and middle aged politicians opined that housewives followed by working women show more interest to PBs. However the middle aged politicians in their second preference viewed working women and youth showing equal interest to PBs. Deviating from this trend, elders found more interest for PBs among youth followed by housewives and working women. This not only justifies their earlier response about men but also shows the consistency in their conceptions about audience. Perhaps they might be under the impression that young women (youth) generally are more exposed to outside world compared to housewives and are more aware of civic affairs relatively. Once again among the elders 19% have not responded to this question.

A similar response was found in rural urban categorisation also. Seniors rated urban masses to be more positive to political messages through media. Contrary to this the other two groups thought rural masses to be so.

The analysis revealed that elders differed with others in their outlook. The responses clearly reflected their clarity and consistency of thought, a sign of maturity that grows with age.

Positionwise, ministers found the rural masses to be highly knowledgeable to appreciate Broadcast media campaigning than the other group. Ministers considered labour class women as having more interest in PBs whereas non-ministers did not find such enthusiasm in them for PBs and instead identified housewives as serious audience. However the difference in this particular aspect is of less significance.

Individual Opinions

Some individual observations expressed in this context are reproduced as below. The type of audience exposed to PB's depends mostly on the quality and contents of the programme—one leader opined, "With the present standard of education in India, the effect of party broadcasts will be only marginal" is another valid observation. "Categories of people who generally do not attend public meetings of political campaigns, non- committed voters and people who are usually confined to their homes show more interest in party broadcasts", one respondent remarked. However, personal contact with the voters is the best way of communication, is another suggestion.

The overall conceptions of the political leaders on the audience can be summed up in the following broad conclusions.

Rural masses are moderately knowledgeable to appreciate the media campaigning. Heavy viewers are likely to get more influenced by these broadcasts than medium and light viewers. Intellectuals among men and housewives among women pay more attention to party broadcasts.

According to a majority, voters with general interest in politics evince more enthusiasm in party broadcasts. By and large, majority of the leaders felt rural masses to be more positive to political messages through Radio/TV than urban. However partywise difference was observed in these two aspects.

Influence of age on the responses was observed to be quite significant. Elders differed with others showing high level consistency in their conceptions about the audience. The administrative position of the sample however has little influence on two aspects.

During discussions it was felt that the sample are not truly aware of the subtle differences among their target audience. Most of them appeared to guess their behaviour and interests. This may partly be due to their limited exposure to the broadcast media campaigning Although well aware of the voters' behaviour, they could not relate it to audience behaviour satisfactorily.

REFERENCES

1. Rose, Richard and McAllister, Ian; *Voters begin to choose : From closed class to open elections in Britain.* London, Sage Publications, 1986, p. 150.
2. Sharada, P.V. ; *Impact of Television on Political Awareness of Rural Masses.* New Delhi, Gyan Publishing House, 1992, pp. 122 and 174.
3. Blumler, Jay G., *The Political Effects of Mass Communication, The Audience Unit-8.* The Open University Social Sciences, a third level course, Milton Keyness, Walton Hall, p.152.

Chapter 7

IMPROVEMENTS IN THE PRESENT SET-UP

The most crucial stage of a party broadcast is its preparation. Who should address the voters? How to convey the message? What are the broadcasting tools and techniques to be used? Is it a simple matter of presentation or does it require any special skills? An observation of the nature of PBs may provide answers to some of these questions.

Campaigning through Radio/TV has three main stages : Planning, Production and Presentation. Some of these aspects were covered in the first part of the study where effort was made to know the merits and demerits of the present system. Others are discussed now to explore the possible improvement in the present set-up and to elicit ideas and suggestions for making more purposeful and effective programmes.

The effectiveness of the campaign ultimately lies in the preparation and presentation of the programme, which involve application of technology. Talking about recording techniques Gamble and Gamble[1] say :

> "Making a sound recording no longer means setting up a microphone and singing a song onto a tape or a record. Recording today has become a contemporary art of self-expression. In recording studios, feelings and emotions are merged with technology; they become one. When working with musicians and producers, the recording engineer uses recording tape as his or her canvas, and music, microphones, mixers, limiters, equalizers,

sound generators and other technological tools as paint brushes".

While these observations broadly explain the production technique of audio programmes, preparation of visual programmes is a still more difficult process requiring additional tools and skills. Since inception, till date, no major change has been introduced in the programme pattern of our political broadcasts. Considerable difference would be noticed at global level in the propaganda through Radio/TV. In some countries, the programmes are transmitted round the clock in different formats like debates, discussions, advertizing, so on and so forth. Public opinion polls provide the necessary feedback for changes in the programmes. Why are we still following the old pattern of programming when many other alternatives are available? Is it because the other models do not suit our requirements? Or because the existing pattern needs no change? Or because no attempt was made to collect the opinions of different cross-sections in this regard other than the audience? What do the leaders have to say in these matters? This part of the study examines the perceptions of politicians and collected suggestions for the changes within the existing set-up.

Opportunity for Unrecognised Political Parties and Independents

On the prospect of providing broadcast opportunity to the above groups over Radio and TV, 76% of the sample, viewed negatively (Table No. 7.1) and explained the problems that may arise with such a practice. Among the 24% who were agreeable some favoured the facility to all political parties but not to the independents and some questioned "why not independents too?" Party-wise BJP was unanimous in saying "No" (i.e. 100%). It may be recalled here that at the time of introducing party broadcasts over Radio/TV, some independent candidates challenged these programmes as discriminatory. However, the courts did not uphold the protest.[2]

TABLE NO. 7.1 : **Distribution of Responses on giving Opportunity to Unrecognized Political Parties and Independents in Party Broadcasts (Q. No. 23).**

Party		*Yes*	*No*	*Total*
Congress (I)	Fre	14	36	50
	%	28	72	-
T.D.P.	Fre	7	18	25
	%	28	72	-
B.J.P.	Fre	-	10	10
	%	-	100	-
Communist	Fre	2	8	10
	%	20	80	-
Others	Fre	1	4	5
	%	20	80	-
Total	Fre & %	24	76	100

There was a progressive increase with agc in the opposition to the suggestion signifying some practical thinking of elders compared to the younger group. The junior politicians might not have thought of the nonfeasibility of such a suggestion in their enthusiasm for new ideas. A minor segment (24%) which favoured extension of the facility to the unrecognized political parties and independents also perhaps, might have said without taking into consideration the facts such as accommodating a huge number of contestants in 2 rounds on Radio/TV etc. The unanimous "no" of BJP shows its firm conviction about the nonpracticability of the suggestion and perhaps even their preference for ideology in politics.

One respondent was emphatically against extending opportunity to the independents in the party broadcasts. Another went a step ahead stating that they should not be allowed to contest the election itself. "All political parties whether recognised or unrecognized may be given the opportunity but certainly not the independents" was another opinion.

Formats for Party Broadcasts

At present the party broadcasts over Radio and TV are in the form of a talk. A chosen person from each party will present a script approved by the media. What are the opinions of politicians in this regard? Are they satisfied with the present format? Or do they prefer any other kind? Among 5 alternative forms of broadcasts suggested, "voters' court" (candidates will be questioned by selected audience) was rated first (25.77%) followed by "debate between the candidates" (23.71%), talk (20.61%), interview (16.49%) and panel discussion (13.40%) (Table No. 7.2). Though the difference is very small between the first-three preferences, many of them felt "voters' court" as the best format for party broadcasts. The voters should be chosen from different cross-sections of the society, they suggested. Some of the sample desired experimenting with all the formats alternatively. One suggestion received in this regard was, instead of one speaker per one round, more participants from each party may be provided opportunity in different formats so that they will get exposure and publicity through media. Party-wise, Congress (I) preferred debate between the candidates (28.57%) followed by interview (20.40%) and voters' court (18.36%).

The existing format in PBs 'talk' and the other two 'interview' and 'discussion' which are generally used for political programming were not given much score by the representatives. Evidently the majority is not in favour of the existing presentation technique of PBs. Talks are monotonous, dull and uninteresting, they said. Since the programme format as such does

TABLE NO. 7.2 : **Distribution of Responses on the Formats for Party Broadcasts (Q. No. 24)**

Party		*Talk*	*Inter-view*	*Panel discus-sion*	*Voters court (Candidates are quest-ioned by selected voters)*	*Debate between the candi-dates*	*Total*
Congress (I)	Fre	8	10	8	9	14	49
	%	16.32	20.40	16.32	18.36	28.57	-
T.D.P.	Fre	5	3	2	9	5	24
	%	21.73	12.5	8.33	37.5	21.57	-
B. J. P.	Fre	2	2	-	4	2	10
	%	20	20	-	40	20	-
Communist	Fre	2	-	2	3	2	9
	%	22.22	-	22.22	33.33	22.22	-
Others	Fre	3	1	1	-	-	5
	%	60	20	20	-	-	-
Total	Fre	20	16	13	25	23	97
	%	20.61	16.49	13.40	25.77	23.71	-

not involve any policy matters, the producers can welcome/introduce new techniques and evolve different types of campaigning programmes using their imagination—they opined.

Ruling out the difficulties involved in the production of such programmes, the politicians felt that many foreign models can be adopted. They pointed out that the listeners and viewers would feel excited to watch a campaign with conflicting and divergent articulations and debate rather than a one sided presentation which usually misleads the voters. An observation by Radclife quoted by Boyd[3] may be of some interest here.

> "Too much of what I see is press release broadcasting. You automatically go and get a ministry, then somebody from the opposition. All these people do is give you party political statements. I find that boring and cannot believe the public learns anything. You already know what the political parties are going to say and I cannot see where any of that does a damn thing to improve the quality of our understanding".

Supporting this observation the respondents suggested that Radio/TV officials should dispense with "playing safe method" in political programming and venture new moves which include divergent thinking/conflict within the available facilities. This may perhaps motivate politicians to depend more on media and contribute to the qualitative and creative political programme production in the near future. An insight into the observations made regarding the nature of formats on foreign media may disclose something worth considering in this direction.

Interview is the most popular conventional format in media programmes. The British Ex-Prime Minister Edward Heath's views on this technique quoted by Cockerell[4] briefs the nature of political interviews presented on British Broadcast media.

> "What I find infinitely boring is when a questioner keeps on and on about the same subject, when you have already told him "no", and that is incompetence by the interviewer not by the person who is answering. Television interviewers tend to respond that most politicians are so slippery that they have to put the same question in, three or four different ways in an attempt to elicit the answer. Our system is inquisitorial with the interviewer there to make clear to everybody that he is much cleverer than the politician he is

> interviewing. So you have to be quite clear in advance as to what you want to say and what you want the audience to hear—why don't we just have a civilized discussion". Explaining further Cockerell says, "For his part, Heath compared the British style of political interviewing unfavourably to his experience in the United States. He felt that American interviewers "acted as impresarios" trying to bring out the different qualities of the person they were interviewing". Heath had come to believe that TV interviews were specifically designed to degenerate into rough houses. But he felt the great snag was that you cannot televise an idea. So the tendency was for ideas to be televised in the form of an argument, therefore, you had these endless confrontations. Heath's political secretary wrote "the divine right of interviewers to govern a discussion is not absolute".

Sometimes interviews focus attention on personalities rather than on enlightening the policies. But this was observed in other formats also where leaders were given airtime in events featured in daily bulletins. The advantage interview has compared to other formats is its probing nature. Some think interviews help audience to understand, assess and compare not only policy distinctions but the leaders' ability to work effectively with those policies as they are spelled out from the horse's mouth. However there were also doubts whether questioning is the best way of clarifying issues. According to some, people do not listen to interviews and words; they watch them; the reactions of the politicians and the way they answer questions.

There is a relationship between the content to be presented and the selection of the format. Choosing a wrong format may distort the message intended to be conveyed. The sample preferred "voters' court" as the most suitable format for election campaigning over Radio/TV. Live audience programming (recently introduced on Indian TV) shows resemblance to the proposed voters' court. This kind of format provides opportunity to elicit information not only from politicians but also the experts. Experiences over foreign media revealed that sometimes the participating public bring more interesting and relevant aspects of the context to the screen through their queries compared to professional broadcasters who sometimes concentrate more on personalities than the issues.

In a Broadcast while content is the matter, format is the form. A wise Broadcaster always selects the suitable format that supplements his purpose. Experimenting with formats brings novelty to the programmes providing opportunity for more audience participation.

Agewise, middle aged group favoured 'voters court' while youngsters thought 'talk' as an ideal format. For debate between the candidates the distribution was equal. It is surprising to note junior generation not giving a thought for any innovative outlook in the technical element of PBs. However, the reason for their selection of conventional format could be the apprehension that other types of presentations may create scope for partisan feelings or it could be a casual response without much thought.

Positionwise the groups have shown slight difference in their preferences. Though voters' court was given more weightage, non-ministers' contribution to this score was higher than the other group. Ministers favoured 'panel discussion' more than that of non-ministers. This perhaps may be because of the reason that in voters' court the possibility of direct attack will be more on the ministers being responsible for implementation of the welfare schemes etc. than on the opposition members (who always talk as if they are representing the public view).

Talk is the most suitable format for party broadcasts; the participants may quarrel and argue and contradict in other forms of programmes—one individual felt.

Party Symbol

Though no one is expected to vote merely on the basis of a symbol, in a country where illiterates are more, symbols do convey some messages. Ballot papers are crowded with numerous names of candidates and party symbols. At the final stage of elections such a huge ballot might confuse the electoral mass. To avoid this confusion familiarizing the symbol is the only way out for achieving the objective. Hence the importance of symbol in elections has its own place especially in a country like India where a new party is emerging every alternate day. When asked whether the symbol of the party should be given prominence in party broadcasts, 46% felt it as necessary, 26% necessary to some extent and 28% not necessary (Table No. 7.3). Partywise, TDP and BJP showed more interest for allowing the symbol to go on air.

A minority group in Cong (I) and Communist parties asserted that established parties are not bothered about such small aspects of campaigning and only new parties need publicity for their symols. But others argued that even for old parties, new voters need to know the symbol and it can be effectively imprinted on the minds of the illiterate voters (who are not aware of the candidate or the party ideology), if sufficient publicity is given during campaigning. On the whole the sample opined that publicity to symbol is definitely an added advantage to them.

TABLE NO. 7.3 : **Distribution of Responses on the Need for giving Prominence for Party Symbol in Party Broadcasts (Q.No. 25)**

Party		*Necessary*	*Necessary to some extent*	*Not neces-sary*	*Don't know*	*Total*
Congress (I)	Fre	18	16	16	—	50
	%	36	32	32	—	—
T.D.P.	Fre	14	4	7	—	25
	%	56	16	28	—	—
B.J.P.	Fre	7	2	1	—	10
	%	70	20	10	—	—
Communist	Fre	4	3	3	—	10
	%	40	30	30	—	—
Others	Fre	3	1	1	—	5
	%	30	10	10	—	—
Total	Fre & %	46	26	28	—	100

Elders during discussion were very particular that symbol need not be given prominence in PBs. However the difference in the scores was marginal. They might be under the impression that additional publicity to this minor aspect may not add much to their benefit in the electoral battle.

Non-ministers wanted to attach prominence to symbol in party Broadcasts. The reason is obvious as the ruling party symbol is quite popular and for other parties any kind of publicity will be advantageous in the elections.

Political Advertising

Political advertising over Radio and T.V. is yet to commence in India, although not a new phenomenon elsewhere. This is a form of persuasion. The new development in this aspect is the broadcast of jingles for short duration. It is observed that in view of the effective presentation styles these spots have become popular in election compaigns and the parties are spending more money on advertising especially over T.V. Since the political spots or jingles are not broadcast over Radio and Television, it is not possible to assess their effect in Indian context. When the respondents were asked to give their opinion a majority (49.49%) said the effect would be 'somewhat' followed by 'not much' (36.36%) and only 13.13% guessed it would be 'very much' (Table No.7.4). While Congress (I) and TDP are the main contributors to these figures, BJP favoured political jingles as it felt the effect would be 'very much' (40%) and the Communists attached more score to 'not much' (55.55%) followed by 'somewhat' (44.44%). Though the leaders agree that the impact of political jingles will be quite impressive, they are afraid of rich parties grabbing more opportunity in this system and some felt it is not advisable. A few have even termed it as an unhealthy practice and felt that Indian masses are not yet mentally prepared for such kind of propaganda.

TABLE NO. 7.4 : **Distribution of Responses on the Effectiveness of Political Advertisement (Q. No. 26)**

Party		*Very much*	*Somewhat*	*Not much*	*Don't know*	*Total*
Congress (I)	Fre	7	23	19	1	50
	%	14	46	38	2	—
T.D.P.	Fre	2	15	8	—	25
	%	8	60	32	—	—
B.J.P.	Fre	4	4	2	—	10
	%	40	40	20	—	—
Communist	Fre	—	4	5	—	9
	%	—	44.44	55.55	—	—
Others	Fre	—	3	2	—	5
	%	—	60	40	—	—
Total	Fre	13	49	36	1	99
	%	13.13	49.49	36.36	1.01	—

A wide range of difference in response was seen between the parties regarding political advertising.

Though not a complete denial, response to this aspect was not encouraging, perhaps because the party managers were concerned about the perverted nature of information flow in commercial broadcasts. However, BJP wanted political advertising to be introduced on an experimental basis and visnalised the effect to be 'very much'. TDP and Cong (I) which have not shown much inclination and the Communists who negated the idea feared that money might play a dominant role in this regard. Those who favoured this idea felt that with proper rules and regulations, this danger can be avoided and the idea may be given a chance at least experimentally. They were also under the strong impression that negating a proposal on pre-conceived notions before implementation is not advisable and experimentation always involves certain amount of risk.

Obviously youngsters' response in this area was more positive compared to the other groups. One would expect middle aged politicians also to show more interest in view of their high involvement in the present day politics. The fears discussed earlier on commercials might also be the reasons for the mild response from the 2nd and 3rd age groups. Positionwise ministers expected the effect of political advertizing to be very much and gave relatively more marks.

Many individual opinions were expressed in this regard. One respondent said that political jingles are welcome if they are free of cost; otherwise must be discouraged. The advertisement rate could be reasonably low, another suggested. With political advertisement, campaigning would become costlier and burdensome where only a section of the polity can afford to participate in the campaigning, one leader feared. Advertizing should be simple to the extent required otherwise people may get bored ; selling of parties makes politics a cheap affair hence an unwarranted idea—these were some of the opinions expressed during the interaction.

The discussion can be concluded with Laver's[5] observation which seems supporting the fears of the representatives on commercial spots.

> " Everyone knows that government departments and other large bodies employ public relations professionals who pasteurize their product to ensure that its consumption poses no risk to their employer's political health. Everyone knows that the media employ the skills of advertising to paint attractive faces on the images they create. Advertising has diminished the credibility of information which is put before the public. Oddly enough, its very power to gather and process vast amounts of public information, and to select and present a chosen but tiny fraction of it as if it were the whole, may end by engendering habits of inattention and scornful disbelief".

Visuals in Party Telecasts

The study reveals that many of the respondents do not recognise much difference in the party broadcasts between Radio and TV except viewing of the personalities on the screen. They expect TV to do a better job than merely presenting the contestants on the small screen. Do our sample have any specific opinions on how TV can present such programmes more effectively?

Analysis shows that 75.51% of the sample felt visuals on TV in support of the messages are of great advantage to them during party broadcasts, but nearly one-fourth of the representatives (24.48%) found them not of much use (Table No. 7.5). However, BJP and TDP preferred the visuals more (90% and 88%) while the Communists were equally divided.

TABLE NO. 7.5 : **Distribution of Responses on the Use of Visuals and Films in Party Broadcasts (Q. No. 27)**

Party		*Yes*	*No*	*Total*
Congress (I)	Fre	35	14	49
	%	71.42	28.57	—
T.D.P.	Fre	22	3	25
	%	88	12	—
B.J.P.	Fre	9	1	10
	%	90	10	—
Communists	Fre	5	4	9
	%	55.55	44.44	—
Others	Fre	3	2	5
	%	60	40	—
Total	Fre	74	24	98
	%	75.51	24.48	—

A large section of the sample (75.52%) supported innovative changes in the formats by preferring incorporation of visual support to party broadcasts. In its negative response, Congress (I) did not visualise any additional advantage of such practice immediately. During interviews the other parties expressed fear that the ruling party might take advantage by showing films of developmental activities of the government, particularly involving the ministers and ruling party leaders. They also expressed the anxiety that some parties may even choose films depicting violence especially those shot during communal riots etc to defame rival candidates.

Normally visual effect promotes better understanding. But the leaders' apprehensions (eventhough minority opinions) bring out the nature of the medium's (TV) visual coverage of political events.

A visual should be used to supplement the content. But unfortunately many observe the domination of visual coverage pushing the content backward. Commenting on British Television's political coverage of 1983 general elections, Maya[6] says,

> "In the search for colour, movement and good visuals, TV coverage has paid increasing attention to the horse-race aspects of contests; of course such factors as changing party strategy, the deployment tactics, the relative size of crowds, polls of the polls, the race for second place, are much of the stuff of which TV election campaigns are made. All the same, broadcasters should take some warning from their American counterparts who in the 1976 persidential campaign devoted two-thirds of their entire coverage to very superficial features of the horse-race variety and less than one-third to issues and policies."

There is a feeling that a well written script or an organised forum over media can do full justice to the topic during crisis. In contrast the present form of election coverage over TV is only superficial service to information mongers. In addition to many other aspects election is also a clash of arguments. Politicians give inspiring speeches during elections. But in Radio and TV coverages they are cut short into one or two minutes with a commentary over the original recording. While media have time limitation many thinkers feel the films of politicians climbing in and out of cars, trains and aeroplanes may dominate the coverage of election campaign neglecting their speeches which are the major source of information for voters to clarify doubts on many issues. Even though the election coverage of Indian Radio/TV has not yet reached the stage to face such criticism this can be seen in the day-to-day coverage of political events.

Agewise youngsters' response to this aspect is more positive than the others.

Analysis of Party Broadcasts

A large number (88%) desired that in future party broadcasts should be followed by an analysis or discussion by eminent thinkers. About 12% who did not like the idea thought that this might create bias among the electorates (Table No. 7.6). The mean scores (Table No.7.7) show that an analysis of party manifesto was liked by many followed by analysis of political leadership and general analysis of party broadcasts. The politicians stressed the need to introduce more of such programmes over Radio and Television. Partywise no noticeable difference was seen.

The sample's preference for the analysis of party manifesto indicates their acknowledgement, indirect though, of the role of media in making masses aware of the issues, and providing a forum for discussion. The effects of such programmes can be visualised from the results of studies carried out earlier to prove the agenda-setting-theory. According to this theory, a member of the audience exposed to a given medium's agenda will adjust his or her perceptions of the importance of political issues in a direction corresponding to the amount of attention paid to those issues in the medium used. However as Blumler[7] opines attempts to test this hypothesis run into problems when there is little difference between communication sources on the issues treated and stressed. At any given political moment, the majority of newspapers, Television bulletins and radio commentaries may all give priority to the same set of issues. In such a case there will be no variance to observe.

However, some studies gave strength to agenda setting theory. One such study as quoted by Blumler is during the American Presidential elections of 1972 conducted by McLeod, Becker and Byrness (1974) in a city (Madison, Wisconsin) which was served by two rather different newspapers—one quite conservative in outlook, the other more liberal in persuasion. A content analysis of the issues mentioned in their campaign stories confirmed the investigators' impression that their election agendas were in fact different. It was observed that the findings of the study gave definite support to the agenda setting hypothesis.

TABLE NO. 7.6 : **Distribution of Responses as to Whether the Future Party Broadcast to be Followed by Experts' Analysis (Q. No. 39)**

Party		*Yes*	*No*	*Total*
Congress (I)	Fre	44	6	50
	%	88	12	—
T.D.P.	Fre	21	4	25
	%	84	16	—
B.J.P.	Fre	10	—	10
	%	100	—	—
Communist	Fre	9	1	10
	%	90	10	—
Others	Fre	4	1	5
	%	80	20	—
Total	Fre & %	88	12	100

One respondent made an observation that many a time, media would take keen interest in selecting suitable participants (speakers) but fail in organising the forum effectively. Stressing the need for rational and scientific approach in programme production, he also suggested continuous evaluation of programmes with the help of feedback. A special note about the role of research in these programmes may not be out of context here. Application of research makes broadcasting more meaningful. Research provides new dimension to the programming and promotes objectivity in broadcasts. There is a notion that research denotes scientific outlook and creativity as an intuitive thinking, something beyond reason and logic hence both may not go together. But many do not accept this argument. While research need not be applied blindly for all categories of programmes, its absence also makes many educational programmes incomplete and unauthentic. Research both at planning and evaluation level should be made a regular exercise in broadcasting. Ofcourse the role of audience research need not be emphasized here. According to Wober *et al.*[8], three topics exist on which audience researchers can usefully provide information in election context. "One is to show to what extent people have encountered the broadcast campaign by measuring what they have seen and heard on TV and Radio. Secondly, public knowledge about party policies and perceptions of issues can be assessed, and sectors of the public where knowledge is lacking can be identified. Thirdly, an attempt can be made to relate the results on patterns of use of the mass media to evidence on interest in issues, knowledge of policies and voting intentions and behaviour".

TABLE NO. 7.7 : **Distribution of Responses on the Type of Analysis for Party Broadcasts (Q. No. 39)**

Party		*Analysis of party Broad-casts*	*Analysis of party Manifesto*	*Analysis of politi-cal Leader-ship*	*Any other opinion (Please specify)*
Congress I	% responded	36	72	58	10
	Mean score	2	1.16	2.13	3
T.D.P.	% responded	28	76	56	24
	Mean score	2.28	1.21	1.92	0.16
B.J.P.	% responded	20	100	60	—
	Mean score	2.5	1	2.16	—
Communists	% responded	40	90	40	—
	Mean score	2.25	1.11	2	—
Others	% responded	80	80	80	
	Mean score	2.5	1	1	—

Each broadcaster can make use of research at his own level for which he need not be a professional researcher. Certain techniques like pre-testing of programmes, evaluation procedures, analysis of feed-back can be learnt through training to the extent required. The broadcasters should realise the advantages of scientific approach in programme production. Unless the long gap between research and the actual field is bridged real development cannot take place in any area. Application of research promotes organised thinking among the broadcasters which in turn reflects in the programming. Eventhough we do not have analysis of party broadcasts on Radio/ TV at present, the available data shows that the production of such programmes especially when parties are in collation is a difficult task. Many feel that the concept of alliance is difficult for voters to grasp. Hence the role of a broadcaster is to make voters understand the policies of different parties and their alliance, joint leadership etc. This is not easily understandable to illiterate voters especially in a political atmosphere where unknown and new issues cropup everyday. Even if media can influence the voting decisions or not it can certainly help them by feeding programmes with the help of politicians and enlighten them about the situation.

Twelve per cent of the leaders have not shown any interest in the analytical programmes. They were sceptical about the free media which normally believe in consumerism. According to them this kind of autonomy may distort the picture neglecting genuine popular views and governments' sensitivities.

Analysis of political leadership in party broadcasts was rated third by the respondents. The contribution of elders to this figure appears to be a bit low. Leadership is an important aspect of politics even-though it secured the last place compared to the other two alternatives i.e., analysis of party manifesto and a general analysis of party broadcasts which secured first and second positions respectively. The slight deviation in response of the elders here is thought provoking. Apart from attaching less importance to the analysis of political leadership in PBs it appears they are not happy with the type and quality of present leadership in general compared to good old times. Most of the senior politicians interviewed were part of the independence movement and had close association with the national leaders of the past. During personal discussion some of the elders criticized the politically immature, disintegrated and inexperienced leadership imposed on parties at times. They have also expressed their inability in improving the present conditions being advanced in age their outlook being considered outdated.

Analysis of party broadcasts in a separate programme may lead to partisan feelings, one leader remarked. Another respondent suggested a detailed model for programming. Further explaining he said that the methodology adopted should be under three distinct categories: each party to explain its manifesto, discussion and debate between the contenders or the party representatives, and final and important one, a party spokesman to answer questions raised by the selected voters.

Guidance for PBs

Hitherto the discussion has been carried out from the media angle based on the responses. There are few aspects that require attention from the politicians' side in preparing the PBs. While the nature of PBs vary from country to country depending on the system it adopts, parties and politicians always put some efforts to make these programmes more effective and purposeful. Few questions were posed to the sample to collect their opinions in this regard.

Generally election broadcasts are prepared on the basis of the guidance and suggestions of some of the party members. In some countries, politicians seek the help of media researchers and special agencies for achieving effective presentation as they consider these programmes to be a major factor contributing to success in elections. When asked whose guidance they sought before preparing a party broadcast, the sample quoted party leaders and party workers followed by listeners and viewers (Table No. 7.8). Media researchers scored pretty low, probably due to the less dependence of our politicians on party broadcasts and scarcity and poor awareness of research in the area concerned. A slight contradiction can be observed here. The sample preferred discussion with the party members before giving a party broadcast leaving the second place to listeners and viewers. They were rather indifferent to and pleaded ignorance of any role of media researchers. But the source from where they collect the opinions of listeners and viewers is not clear. Also, the sample do not seem to have considered the subtle distinction between voters and listeners/ viewers. They appeared to be quite sure about the voter's psychology and are under the impression that the interests and opinions of listeners/viewers can be well assessed by them. This is not only unscientific but also shows their lack of awareness about the activities of media researchers, thus indicating the poor appreciation and application of research in political communication.

It is observed, politicians sometimes employ market research organizations to know the intentions of voters or to confirm their opinions about the voting behaviour. Political parties show great interest in collecting and analysing the data not only to know voters' opinion about their policies and programmes but also their response to other parties' activities. This provides feed-back enabling them to change their strategies

TABLE NO. 7.8 : **Distribution of Agencies whose Guidance is sought before giving Party Broadcasts (Q. No. 10).**

Party		*Media Researchers*	*Listeners/ Viewers*	*Intellectuals*	*Party Leaders/ Party Workers.*
Congress I	% responded	52	60	78	88
	Mean score	2.42	2.06	2.12	1.70
T.D.P.	% responded	36	24	88	96
	Mean score	3.11	2.23	2.45	1.37
B.J.P.	% responded	40	40	60	80
	Mean score	3.25	1.25	2.16	2.12
Communists	% responded	20	80	30	90
	Mean score	3.5	1.5	3	1.66
Others	% responded	40	80	60	100
	Mean score	3	2.25	2.33	1

and plan new programmes. Since winning an election is not an easy task, many techniques of research are being applied in this direction and new models were developed to assess the attitudes and perceptions of voters in advance before elections. This trend can be seen in Indian election context also. Many media organizations especially newspapers conduct pre-election polls and publish the findings. These findings are proved to be correct sometimes, but not always. Opinion polls have created interest among the political media researchers to study the possible effect of their findings on the votings behaviour. The following observations may show the potential of these polls as an influencing factor during elections. According to Gamble and Gamble[9] these polls serve as the scorers of the races until election day when the public actually chooses a winner. Good poll ratings will help a candidate to be taken seriously while a low standing in the polls can drive one out of the race. The opinion polls can also help to create a candidate. But Dr. Robert Waller's observation at Harris as quoted by Walter Debbie[10] is that the polls measure an unpriced vote, and attitude rather than expected behaviour, and that once in the polling booth, the voter attach a price to his vote which then impacts on his choice. Explaining the undesirable political consequences that may develop due to the opinion polls, Laver[11] says,

> Undecided voters who would like to feel that they are on the winning side may leap on to a band wagon. Conversely, those anxious not to waste their votes may desert a predicted loser. Should the polls suggest that a party will win by a handsome margin, its lazier or more apathetic supporters may not take the trouble to vote. Timid electors may back-pedal and refrain from voting for a party expected to win easily in order to preserve it from the arrogance that goes with having too dominant a majority in the assembly. Tactical voting may take place where there is more than one opposition party:Voters are then cast to defeat rather than to elect, and opponents who usually support party "C" switch their votes to party "B" in the hope of defeating the even more disliked party "A". Tactical voting is not likely to be effective without the knowledge of party positions revealed by opinion polls".

Another observation in this context is the findings of opinion polls just before the recent presidential election (November 1992) in America. Quoting James Lengle, Bhagvan Singh[12] says "Personality and perceived strength of leadership have come to overshadow party loyalty in American politics. And the three TV debates between President Bush and

Challenger Clinton could be decisive for the outcome of the results. Pollsters point out that in a TV debate, the younger and charismatic Clinton with his proven debating skills is likely to overshadow the tired looking old man Bush. The TV debates have a vast reach of 100 million Americans at one go". (published on October 18th 1992).

Laver[13] also supports the above contentions. According to him 'information technologies, combination of televised debates and interviews with opinion polling have also emphasized the influence of the public 'images' of parties and politicians. To this extent he quotes an experienced British parliamentarian Micheal Foot, who deplored the domination of "politics of perception" over the "politics of persuasion". But today Laver says persuasion is more commonly achieved by image building than by rational argument.

In conclusion it can be said—whether the opinion polls are effective in predicting the voters behaviour or not they are certainly giving some feed-back to the politicians and public and creating an atmosphere of private polls. Whether they are helping the parties to change their strategies and public to adjust their voting intentions or not but have become an important aspect of pre-election activity.

Eventhough a recent phenomenon in Indian election scene, the effect of these opinion polls can be assessed from the above observations. However it was also felt that the authenticity of these poll results largely depends on the methodological foundations adopted in collecting the data such as the size of the sample, whether they represent different cross-sections or not, techniques used for data collection, issues covered, the samples knowledge about political matters, how serious the researchers and sample (i.e. whether the surveys are conducted with commercial outlook or genuine inquisitiveness) etc.

Selecting the Candidate

Each party consists of many leaders. How do they select a person for party broadcast? According to Cong (I) and TDP popularity among the general public was claimed to be the major qualification in selecting a person, whereas for BJP it is standing in the party. However, Communists preferred both the merits equally (Table No. 7.9). This reflects the generally prevailing dual trend in the political sphere i.e. the party base versus the individual merit.

Oratory and intellectual appeal alone cannot serve the political purposes of broadcasts, they said. The less score given to political oratory may deserve a special note here. Oratory has been considered as one of the important traits of a leader's personality. The relationship between oratory and Radio/TV speeches is inseparable. What made the representatives think that oratory is of less importance for choosing a candidate? In an attempt to study the role of persuasive language in political communication and the need to adopt it to the requirements of a particular medium, Atkinson[14] says :

TABLE NO. 7.9 : **Distribution of Responses on the Selection of Person for Party Broadcasts (Q. No. 11)**

Party		*Oratory*	*Standing in the party*	*Popularity among the public*	*Intellectual appeal*
Congress (I)	% responded	76	68	96	66
	Mean score	2.31	2.47	1.37	2.78
T.D.P.	% responded	72	68	70	72
	Mean score	2.5	2.29	1.33	3
B.J.P.	% responded	60	100	70	60
	Mean score	2.83	1.6	2.28	2.5
Communists	% responded	70	80	90	60
	mean score	3	1.5	1.55	3.33
Others	% responded	80	60	100	60
	Mean score	2.5	1.33	1.6	2.66

"Not only does live oratory remains one of the divers sources of political messages which are communicated to the electorate, but the relative technical competence of individual politicians is still relevant to the development of their public images. At the same time, the present research suggests that some of the historically most effective types of verbal device can be used and may work in a similar way when deployed in the more informal settings where most televised talk now takes place. To this extent, then an understanding and mastery of the traditional skills of oratory may still be of considerable importance when it comes to speaking persuasively on television providing that speakers also have an adequate awareness which of its practices are not readily transferable to the small screen".

The role of oratory in the televised debates of American presidential elections over years need not be highlighted here. Supporting the above observation one respondent said he would prefer to listen/watch a particular politician's speech who is popular for his oratory, when asked whether he listens/watches the Broadcast of leaders of other parties.

Some of the respondents vehemently criticized their leaders for not providing them an opportunity to present the party broadcasts. It is understood they were neither consulted nor even informed about these aspects. They were discontented over the practice and asked what interest and follow-up can be expected from them in these programmes under such circumstances.

Election Promises

There is a general notion that politicians make empty promises to influence the voters especially during election campaigning. On account of this, voters are usually critical of politicians and in turn the leaders face difficulty in convincing the public about their policies and programmes. When asked about the authenticity of this notion, majority of the respondents accepted it as a part of election game (56.12%). While one group claimed it as an occasional exercise (25.51%) another small fraction (8%) felt it a rare phenomenon. But a 10% refuted and remarked that this observation is wrong (Table No. 7.10). While trying to defend, some respondents said neither it is an invention of the present day politics nor the intention of any politician to make empty promises but they are compelled to go for this exercise as a hangover. Moreover, the public also seems to enjoy this kind of boast and vanity—they opined. Explaining further they said that several constraints would be faced later in fulfilling the promises even though they were sincere while promising and great effort will be made to overcome such obstacles. Around 10% of the group (mostly Communist leaders) refuted this argument and felt that politicians make promises with convictions. At this particular question, some politicians felt uncomfortable, some laughed it away, some got angry and some attributed it as true in case of others but not for themselves. Communists claim that politicians never make empty promises. This (22.22%) reflects their general isolation from the main stream and stretching of their commitments to political ideology. In Andhra Pradesh, their strength is very limited (though their ideology is spread over many areas for a long time) and perhaps the idealism could be because they never attained enough strength for entertaining hopes to rule the state.

More members of the above 55 age group, compared to the youngsters (Group I), felt that politicians usually make empty promises. The leaders of this group constituting more number of mature and retired politicians, perhaps are not happy with the persent style of political campaigning and have sincerely accepted the truth. The elders giving low score to

TABLE NO. 7.10 : **Distribution of Responses on the Extent of Empty Promises made in Election Broadcasts (Q. No. 15)**

Party		*Usually*	*Ocassion-ally*	*Rarely*	*Never*	*Total*
Congress (I)	Fre	21	15	6	7	49
	%	42.85	30.61	12.24	14.28	—
T.D.P.	Fre	16	8	—	1	25
	%	64	32	—	4	—
B.J.P.	Fre	8	1	1	—	10
	%	80	10	10	—	—
Communists	Fre	7	—	—	2	9
	%	77.77	—	—	22.22	—
Others	Fre	3	1	1	—	5
	%	60	20	20	—	—
Total	Fre	55	25	8	10	98
	%	56.12	25.51	8.16	10.20	—

"rarely" and "never" on the scale also supports the assessment. Contrary to this, youngsters seem to be unwilling to engage in selfcriticism.

While non-ministers confirmed the practice of politicians making empty promises as occurring usually, ministers brushed it aside as a rare exercise. Here the reason is obvious as non-ministers comprise more opposition members and it is common practice that the opposition parties criticise ministers for failure in fulfilling the promises made during elections.

The tendency of politicians making empty promises, one legislator thought, depends on the personality of the politician and there is no set pattern. It varies from person to person according to the reputation and credibility he or she enjoys among the voters. Another remarked that the party's performance and reputation also have a contribution in this regard. Responsible political parties will be more cautious and careful in such matters; parties and individuals who are not sure of winning the race will resort to such unhealthy parctices. Some legislators remarked that the masses have a right to seek explanation from the politicians for their failure in keeping up the promises.

Findings of this part thus indicate that the partymen desire changes in the present set-up except in the denial of opportunity to unrecognised political parties and independents. They made reasonable suggestions for better presentation of election appeals over Radio/TV—and were straight forward in expressing their hopes, doubts and apprehensions about many aspects such as advertising, use of visuals etc. To sum up, the leaders selected voters' court followed by debate between the candidates as suitable formats for election broadcasts. More prominence to party symbol and visual support to presentations were also suggested though they differed partywise. Political advertizing did not receive much support except from one party. The programmes should include analysis of party manifestos—they opined. The representatives felt that the suggestions of the party leaders and workers should be sought before preparing political broadcasts. While some parties considered popularly among the public as a pre-requisite in choosing the person for broadcast for some standing in the party seems to be the deciding factor.

As regards to the content of the campaigning making empty promises was claimed as a usual practice. Age and position of the sample have shown influence only to some extent.

REFERENCES

1. Gamble, Michael W. and Gamble, Teri Kwal; *Introducing Mass Communication,* Singapore, McGraw Hill Book Company, 1989, p. 177.
2. Baruah, U. L; *This is All India Radio* : New Delhi, Publications Division, Ministry of Information and Broadcasting 1983, p. 172.
3. Boyd, Andrew; *Broadcast Journalism - Techniques of Radio and TV News;* Oxford, Heinmann Professional Publishing Ltd.
4. Cockerell, Michael; Live from No.10; *The Inside Story of Prime Ministers and Television.* London, Faber and Faber Ltd. 1983, pp.173 & 174.
5. Laver, Murray; *Information Technology—Agent of Change,* Cambridge, Cambridge University Press, 1989, p.152.
6. Even, Maya, *Television broardcasting of post-war election* p.27 Crewe, Ivor and Harrop, Martin : *Op. cit.*
7. Blumer, Jay G., *The political effects of Mass-communication,* The Audience Unit 8, The Open University Social Sciences a Third level course, Milton Keyness, Walton Hall, p.30.
8. Wober Mallory ; Svenning Michael; and Gunter, Barrie—*The Television audience and the 1983 general elections,* p. 96. Crewe, Ivor and Harrop, Martin (Ed.) *Political Communications The General Election Campaign of 1983,* Cambridge University Press, 1986.
9. Gamble, Michael W. and Gamble, Teri Kwal: *Op. cit.* p. 401.
10. Walter, Debbie, The polls and polling day; why didn't U.K. voters do what the research samples say they would? "*Admap*" July/August 1992, p. 22.
11. Laver, Murray : *Op. cit.* p.145.
12. Bhagwan Sing, R.; U.S.Election '92; *Deccan Chronicle,* October 18th 1992 (Supplement) Secunderabad, Andhra Pradesh, India.
13. Laver, Murray : *Op. cit,* p. 146.
14. Atkinson, Max, *The 1983 general election and the demise of live oratory.* p. 53.
    Crewe, Ivor and Martin Harrop : *op. cit.*

Chapter 8

SOME PERCEPTIONS ABOUT BROADCAST MEDIA AND POLITICS

As Gamble & Gamble[1] observes "Each new endeavour is a creative effort building on past efforts. A good study opens the door to many new studies". Research has opened new vistas in the development of political communication theory. While early assumptions were reflected in magic-bullet theory of mass communication (the mass media could hit and inject people with messages just as a bullet penetrates its target), two-step flow theory was dominant at the later stages which gave importance to opinion leaders in the communication process. Now the emphasis is more on studying the effects. While the past assumptions were not completely rejected the present trend seems to be in agreement with the magic-bullet theorists i.e., the media can have greater impact. Some of the present day researchers are also of the view that the old theorists are not wrong but the research techniques adopted during those days were not sufficient to measure the influence. They also feel that all these theories are applicable to specific time periods only. These views reflect the need to consider the developments taking place in the field of mass communication at global level before arriving at any conclusion.

Studies on political effects of Radio and Television on audiences have revealed many findings confirming the strength of Broadcast media as an election asset. These findings can be used as searchlights to probe further into the subject. Indian conditions are quite different from the context in which these studies are conducted. However, it was felt that the views and perceptions of the leaders about the role of Broadcast media in party politics could be assessed in greater depth taking into consideration the earlier observations.

The fourth part of the questionnaire was devoted entirely to this assessment and the questions were framed with statements based on known research findings and observations in the field of political communication. The sample appeared to have found this part of the questionnaire somewhat difficult to comprehend at the first glance and most of them responded after careful consideration.

Passive Learning through Media

In the present communication process through mass-media, the audience are passive receivers. While passivity has many disadvantages, it certainly yields good results in the long run. What are the implications of this nature in political education of masses? Mediamen generally say, "In the process of political communication, broadcast media, with its greater reach to the less educated part of the electorate, is likely to promote passive learning and this in the long run may activate the electorate and indirectly help them".

More than half of the politicians (57.14%) supported this observation (Table No. 8.1). For 22.44%, it is not just passive learning since listening promotes thinking thus turning it into an active learning process. The rest (18.36%) considered masses to be intelligent and creative enough to appreciate, analyse and decide future course of action on receiving political messages through the media. According to a very small proportion (2.04%), these broadcasts seldom promote any learning. The figures of active and creative learning put together (40.80%) show the respondents' faith in Radio and Television as political tools. Partywise TDP gave second preference to creative learning (20%) while BJP attached equal importance to both creative and active learning (20% each). Creative learning found more favour with the Communists (30%).

TABLE NO. 8.1 : **Distribution of Responses on the Types of Learning Promoted by Broadcast Media (Q. No. 28)**

Party		*Passive learning (slow learning)*	*Active learning*	*Creative learning*	*No learning at all*	*Total*
Congress (I)	Fre	27	14	6	1	48
	%	56.25	29.16	12.5	2.08	-
T.D.P.	Fre	17	2	5	1	25
	%	68	8	20	4	-
B.J.P.	Fre	6	2	2	-	10
	%	60	20	20	-	-
Communists	Fre	5	2	3	-	10
	%	50	20	30	-	-
Others	Fre	1	2	2	-	5
	%	10	40	40	-	-
Total	Fre	56	22	18	2	98
	%	57.14	22.44	18.36	2.04	-

A fairly positive picture thus emerges on the nature of learning that takes place among the voters through political media both from the partial agreements on passive learning and from the appreciable scores to the higher forms of learning (i.e. active and creative). Elders visualised more of active learning by the audience from the broadcasts and were rather sceptical of creative learning. There appears to be a valid point in the elders' opinion. The word 'creative' has a broader and even deeper meaning. It requires a higher state of mental faculty which cannot be stimulated directly unless the learner already has a minimum knowledge about the subject.

Radio/TV promoting creative learning among the audiences is not a proven fact by the media researchers and also makes one to doubt the possibility of its happening. However, this may be true in case of audience who are already well aware of politics, since creativity also involves giving new dimension to knowledge already acquired. The score given to 'creative learning' also slightly contradicts their own responses to some of the earlier discussed questions. Even though they are sceptical about the present conditions their faith in the power of media in general seems to be high. However, the majority (57.14%) endorsement to television's role in the long run in promoting passive learning among voters substantiates the studies organised earlier in this field. In political context while assessing the media influence usually T.V. is singled out as an important medium. However it is not so always especially when the T.V. is still in infancy and the other media are given more weightage. But certain qualities of T.V. coverage of politics like visuals which make the news more authentic, less interpretation in reporting, popularity among the illiterates, reach etc., many feel help undecided voters to collect information passively without any abtrusion. An American work (1976) quoted by Blumler[2] further explains the crucial role T.V. can play during elections.

> "Along with contributing to the nationalization of electorate TV has opened up the political system. The ease with which information may be acquired about issues, causes and candidates from TV by political unsophisticates may not increase their sense of efficacy or sense of trust but it may well increase their sense of competence to participate

in the political process. But they are only occasional participants. The occasional participant armed with a civic duty conscience that he should participate and a Television instilled confidence that he can participate may be partially responsible for the increasing volatility of the electorate".

Reaching the Unknown Voters

The term broadcasting clearly denotes the pervasive nature of Radio-Television. Its efficacy in covering large areas (including remote tribal areas) has provided the media with additional advantages. Some think that this pervasiveness poses problems in programming. While serving the interests of large masses the media may have to compromise in depth and specialization in the treatment of the subject which may result in superficial and sometimes simple programming.

In the political context, researchers usually feel that "party broadcasts over Radio and Television are reaching a sector of voters who were not approached earlier. As Table 8.2 indicates nearly two-thirds (66%) agreed with this statement while a little below one-fourth (23%) strongly agreed and one out of every ten (10%) was in disagreement. During personal discussions one politician questioned the researcher; "Do you mean to say that people without Radio and Television sets are not aware of the election news?".

Partywise it is noteworthy that only BJP is in cent per cent agreement. One female respondent felt this problem inapplicable to female politicians since they were able to meet women voters in *purdah* system in course of door-to-door campaign and do not find any barriers. On the whole the 89% positive response shows the sample's confidence in Radio and Television as vehicles to reach the unknown voters. BJP's cent per cent agreement here shows its firm belief in the potential of Broadcast media. Among Congress (I) also 90% agreement was seen.

TABLE NO. 8.2 : **Distribution of Responses whether party Broadcasts Reach Voters in Difficult Segments (Q. No. 29)**

Party		*Strongly agree*	*Agree*	*Disagree*	*Strongly disagree*	*Don't know*	*Total*
Congress (I)	Fre	14	31	5	-	-	50
	%	28	62	10	-	-	-
T.D.P.	Fre	5	16	3	-	1	25
	%	20	64	12	-	4	-
B.J.P.	Fre	3	7	-	-	-	10
	%	30	70	-	-	-	-
Communists	Fre	1	7	2	-	-	10
	%	10	70	20	-	-	-
Others	Fre	-	5	-	-	-	5
	%	-	100	-	-	-	-
Total	Fre %	23	66	10	-	1	100

The middle aged group unanimously supported the ability of PBs in reaching the remote voters. Among the youngsters and seniors around 15% expressed doubt in this regard. It may be said that the active leaders (2nd group), eventhough had not derived much advantage from the electronic campaigning, might have observed and assessed the capacity of Radio and TV better than others during the consecutive elections and realised its potentiality in reaching the nook and corner of the country.

Radio and Television as Domestic Media

In clubs/schools/community halls and sometimes in homes also listening to/viewing programmes is a collective activity which will be usually followed by an organized or informal discussion. Collective listening/viewing has many advantages. It minimizes the problem of one way communication and passive listening/viewing. When people watch the same programme together they not only enjoy but the possibility of discussing it further as a shared topic is also more. The study, therefore, included the question, "Broadcast media being a domestic media can bring political messages into the home environment. This may lead to further discussion in the home which may in turn lead to active political participation later. Is this happening now?"

Only 13.5% found it happening a great deal while 73.95% expressed it as only somewhat true and 11.45% "not much" (Table No. 8.3). The sample were cynical about the existing situation but could not altogether deny the possibility of such a change and answered half-heartedly. Partywise, again BJP's response to "great deal" was as high as 30%. The leaders' meagre agreement in this respect may need further examination.

Domestic media has the limitation of low involvement. As Barwise and Ehrenberg[3] observe,

> "there is usually some involvement, in what we watch but mostly it does not go very deep. It is a "low involvement" but not "no involvement". According to them watching Television is a passive activity in two senses. "It involves little physical, emotional, intellectual and financial effort or investment and most of the time, it is something that we do as a filler when we have nothing better or more important to do".

Curiously most of those who felt the power of Radio/TV to be 'not much' in this context were of BJP. Hitherto, BJP has been showing a steady stance on the power of the media. This opinion somewhat contradicts the group's convictions. Or, perhaps their perception of 'active politics' is different and they might believe that the education and knowledge one gains through this media may not necessarily lead

TABLE NO. 8.3 : **Distribution of Responses whether Party Broadcasts are Promoting Discussion in the Homes (Q. No. 30)**

Party		*Great deal*	*Some-what*	*Not much*	*Don't know*	*Total*
Congress (I)	Fre	5	35	6	1	47
	%	10.63	74.46	12.76	2.12	-
T.D.P.	Fre	4	18	3	-	25
	%	16	72	12	-	-
B.J.P.	Fre	3	5	2	-	10
	%	30	50	20	-	-
Communists	Fre	1	8	-	-	9
	%	11.11	88.88	-	-	-
Others	Fre	-	5	-	-	5
	%	-	100	-	-	-
Total	Fre	13	71	11	1	96
	%	13.54	73.95	11.45	1.94	-

one into action. It may be a case of sampling variation also. Communists were evenly divided between 'great deal' and 'somewhat' (99.90%) which gives an impression that they are cent per cent in agreement on the media's role as a political initiator.

Elders did not extend much support to this observation. They attached less score to the category 'great deal' on the scale compared to other groups. A similar view was reflected in the response of middle aged politicians who felt the effect of Radio/TV as 'not much' relatively.

Non-partisan Stance

"The greatest enemies of free, serious, political broadcasting are not the broadcasters but the political leaders themselves. If political programmes or interviews deviate a hair's breadth from what they themselves consider fair, the leaders rise up in wrath"—(Michael Cockerell)[4].

Coverage of election news has always caused concern among the politicians as there is a possibility of influencing the voting intentions in favour of a particular party or candidate. While criticism against the press is more obvious Broadcast media is no less criticised in this respect.

The next question, therefore, sought the agreement of the representatives to a statement : "Broadcast media maintains non-partisan stance in its relationship to party political conflict and maintains fairness, impartiality and neutrality. To what extent do you agree with this image of the media?". Many leaders, especially of BJP and Communist parties, consider that in party broadcasts during elections the electronic media is impartial and neutral, since it gives equal opportunity to all the parties—while not being so in the day-to-day coverage of the party activities during other times. Ruling party grabs most of the coverage in regular news bulletins and this publicity is an additional advantage to the party in power during elections, they explained. Even in party broadcasts also exactly half of the sample (50%) rated it to be non-partisan only "to some extent" followed by more than one-third (35%) "to a great extent" and "not at all" by a small group of 14% (Table No. 8.4). Around 52.50% of the Congress (I) leaders rated "to a great extent" followed by 44% "to some extent". Among the Communists, 40% did not agree with the statement at all.

On the whole the frequencies show the prevailing general dissatisfaction among the politicians about Broadcast media's impartiality in coverage of politics during elections and in between elections. However, politicians manipulating media for their selfish motives were also considered as one of the factors for media's partisan stance irrespective of the fact to which party they belong and whether they are in power or not.

TABLE NO. 8.4 : **Distribution of Responses whether Party Broadcasts Maintain Neutrality (Q. No. 31)**

Party		*To a great extent*	*To some extent*	*Not at all*	*Don't know*	*Total*
Congress (I)	Fre	26	22	2	-	50
	%	52	44	4	-	-
T.D.P.	Fre	5	15	4	1	25
	%	20	60	16	4	-
B.J.P.	Fre	2	6	2	-	10
	%	20	60	20	-	-
Communists	Fre	1	5	4	-	10
	%	10	50	40	-	-
Others	Fre	1	2	2	-	5
	%	20	40	40	-	-
Total	Fre %	35	50	14	1	100

Here a ruling and opposition division is prominently observed, among the respondents. Those who agreed it to be existing "to some extent" only during party broadcasts also felt that the non-controversial diplomatic approach of media personnel is resulting in ineffective programming and making the impartiality and neutrality a meaningless exercise. Cong (I) giving considerable score to "a great extent" and Communists to "not at all"—the reasons are perhaps obvious.

Both above 55 and middle age groups supported broadcast media's non-partisan stance in party politics. Youngsters also confirmed this by attaching low score to 'not at all' on the scale. As discussed earlier the sample felt the media to be biased only during elections. Logically the leaders cannot claim PBs to be partisan during elections because of the equal distribution of time and frequency irrespective of the strengths of the political parties. This perhaps could be the reason for the representatives' positive response so far observed. This also might be the reason behind the seniors and middle aged leaders feeling media to be non-partisan to a great extent during elections. These groups hitherto were critical in assessing the potential of the media.

As usual broadcast media's non-partisan stance in party conflict was challenged by many of the non-ministers who gave slightly higher score to 'not at all' on the scale.

Whether the media is free or in government's control, the criticism of 'bias' in presenting information is a wide-spread fact. While the blame is attributed to ruling party in government controlled media the free media is also prone to such criticism for its pronounced bias by siding with one or other parties. Eventhough the criticism is accepted to a great extent due to many reasons there are some sections which believe the bias to be an inherent nature of the media than generated out of prejudice. They argue—the duration of news items is very short and the number of events that can be reported are also very few. The news value from the view point of a T.V. Producer is different from other media reporters. Stories which produce good pictures, conflict and drama are given more weightage in T.V. coverage. In addition to the significance of news the T.V. reporter also has the responsibility of making it an interesting visual presentation. Usually demonstrations and events involving many people attract viewers than discussion or analytical programmes. Naturally there is a tendency to go for such programmes and time factor again restricts the scope of the programme to a superficial coverage than an in-depth analysis. These limitations are often misunderstood as bias. To this effect Tyrrel[5] quotes Gans who observed.

> "Newsmen, particularly in television, are by experience and training always conscious of the

need for objectivity. A reputation for political prejudice would be damaging professionally. But objectivity itself has its perils. The neutral reporter cannot describe as falsehood what he knows to be a lie. Unless he can find a respected figure to deny a false statement, it must go by default. If he does not report it, it is suppression, and if he denies it himself he has entered into controversy."

Some feel the bias among the reporters is of "unconscious" nature. Even though the journalists are aware of public criticism they are to a large extent helpless. The techniques of news reporting and other circumstances are to some extent responsible for this. However, a conscious bias is also not an impossible task for them but in case of T.V. too many people are to be involved which is practically difficult.

While these opinions represent some views about the problem under discussion they certainly help the broadcasters to know about the limitations of the techniques and tools they use for programming and also make them think to overcome these limitations.

Television as a Political Medium

"Communication researchers opine that television as a political medium occasionally gives publicity boost to less established contenders". Many (68.68%) of the sample were in full agreement with this opinion (Table No. 8.5). About 13.13% strongly agreed and likewise an equal number have disagreed. The last group thought that if a politician is not already a known personality to the electorate their accepting such a person just by a mere watching Television will not arise. TV may give a little boost to people already popular in political circles, they felt. However in general, the potentiality of TV in making people more familiar was accepted by majority of the representatives. Partywise BJP (100%) and TDP (92%) almost totally supported this assessment.

TABLE NO. 8.5 : **Distribution of Responses whether Television Gives Publicity Boost to Less Established Contenders (Q. No. 32)**

Party		*Strongly agree*	*Agree*	*Disagree*	*Strongly disagree*	*Don't know*	*Total*
Congress (I)	Fre	6	30	10	1	3	50
	%	12	60	20	2	6	-
T.D.P.	Fre	4	19	1	-	1	25
	%	16	76	4	-	4	-
B.J.P.	Fre	2	8	-	-	-	10
	%	20	80	-	-	-	-
Communists	Fre	1	6	2	-	-	9
	%	11.11	66.66	22.22	-	-	-
Others	Fre	-	5	-	-	-	5
	%	-	100	-	-	-	-
Total	Fre	13	68	13	1	4	99
	%	13.13	68.68	13.13	1.01	4.04	-

People from all walks of life show great interest to participate in TV programmes, especially those who are in need of publicity. To streamline such enthusiasm, Radio and TV adopt uniform procedures, regulations and policy guidelines which invariably invite criticism. The response in this context clearly depicts the growing influence of television in the political sphere. It may be apt to quote Cockerell[6] who identified the specific character of the medium that is responsible in impressing the audience.

> "It seems most likely that TV works on viewers during elections as it does between campaigns. TV's strength is as a medium of impression rather than analysis. And in the heightened atmosphere of an election campaign it tends not to make miraculous new converts but to confirm prejudices and impressions that have themselves been built up by the small screen in the preceding years".

It may be fitting here to quote Boyd[7] who observes "The Constitution of U.S. does not say that the President of US shall not weigh 300 pounds, but TV says so".

The 13.13% who do not believe that TV gives publicity to less known persons are from Cong (I) and Communists. While Communists disagreement is reasonable the ruling party's response is quite unexpected. Usually ruling party will have more access to official media than others. This naturally gives them an opportunity to make themselves more familiar to voters both physically and intellectually. However, three reasons could be identified for this response—one, the representatives covered by the study (which includes many ministers) might not have received any extra publicity through TV. Another reason could be most of them have started their political career long back and became leaders without any media support. TV is a recent development and especially in political matters it is still in infancy. They might have thought that time is not yet ripe to accord such power to the medium in Indian context. A third may be that they do not wish to concede that TV is indeed trying to popularise less known people. Leftists felt that media is only a means but not a maker. A politician should reach the hearts of the people through his endeavours to become a leader—they opined. Without this quality, no amount of media publicity can help him. Moreover, when a person is already popular it is natural that media gives coverage to him as part of its programme, but not as an offer of favour to boost publicity. According to them media giving publicity to politicians is a wrong notion.

This observation found much favour with youngsters. Only two of them out of 36 (60%) disagreed whereas in the other groups as many as 18.5% disagreed. TV is more promising to youngsters who have a long political career ahead, but for elders the favours TV can bring at the fag end of political life are likely to be meek. These could be the factors responsible for the variations in the responses according to age difference in assessing the capability of the glamorous TV as a political medium.

Political Unsophistication

Some degree of political and behavioural unsophistication is often attributed to voters and politicians alike in our country. It is observed that this makes Broadcast media campaigning and programming a difficult exercise.

While partially agreeing with this observation, the respondents felt that the quality of the production depends on the type of the programme, participants, topic etc. Around 37.11% felt it only "somewhat difficult" whereas an equal number (36.08%) said "it depends" (Table No 8.6) and while 15.46% thought it to be 'very difficult', a bare 11.34% found it not difficult at all. Dismissing it as a minor problem, some claimed that with regular exposure, the problem of unsophistication will not arise and the participating politicians will be more conscious of the restraint aspect of behaviour.

TABLE NO. 8.6 : **Distribution of Responses on the Impact of Political Unsophistication on the Broadcast Media Campaigning (Q. No. 33)**

Party		*Very difficult*	*Somewhat difficult*	*It depends*	*Not difficult at all*	*Total*
Congress (I)	Fre	7	21	17	4	49
	%	14.28	42.85	34.69	8.16	-
T.D.P.	Fre	3	7	11	4	25
	%	12	28	44	16	-
B.J.P.	Fre	2	3	4	1	10
	%	20	30	40	10	-
Communists	Fre	1	3	2	2	8
	%	12.5	37.5	25	25	-
Others	Fre	2	2	1	-	5
	%	40	40	20	-	-
Total	Fre	15	36	35	11	97
	%	15.46	37.11	36.08	11.34	-

Critics feel our politicians are habituated to address large gatherings in public meetings and Parliament etc. The speeches usually designed to hold the attention of big crowds may not come into terms with the requirements of Television audience. This is more so with live broadcast of political events. Another observation is the difference among audience. The crowds in public meetings are usually motivated groups whereas the T.V. viewers are general audience. When the programmes are produced keeping these aspects in view the problem of unsophistication can be minimized to some extent.

The respondents who marked "it depends" and 'not difficult at all' are perhaps under the impression that media personal can avoid such situations with proper planning and good programming. A few said there is no harm if the broadcasts are crude as the voters will have an opportunity to know the real behaviour of the contenders on the screen. Partywise, majority of TDP and BJP said it depends on the programme whereas Cong (I) and Communists found it to be only somewhat difficult.

The party managers low profile about their behaviour, however may not be a permanent feature and may even reverse in future. As Pilsworth[8] warns

> "Television broadcasters have for years been striving to get the parties to understand the requirements of the medium. It is clear that the party managers have learned quickly and have adopted to its on-occasion simplistic demands rather well. Unfortunately, the broadcasters do not now seem to be able to match the parties' new-found sophistication. They must learn to respond to the increasing professionalism of the party managers in the manipulation of news values and the creation of new events".

Around 19% of junior leaders (first and second group) opined politicians' and voters' unsophistication may come in the way of producers in making qualitative political programmes. But the elders have struck off this complaint and for only one out of 26 this appeared to be a problem. This group suggested that the problem can be tackled if producers take proper care and interest.

Ministers reluctantly accepted the observation that the difficulty in media programming is due to politicians' unsophistication. The ministers are more among the respondents who thought that it depends on the type of the programme. Most of the ministers do not see such a problem. The sensitivity of the issues under discussion and lack of professionalism on the part of Broadcasters contribute more to this problem than politicians' unsophistication—they opined. However non-ministers assessed this problem as not so easy to get on. Usually the opposition members while discussing the issues on media turn more emotional and moderators take considerable time to cool them down. The non-ministers' (who comprise more number of opposition members) response raises the doubt whether they are really accepting this as a fact or were only casual in the response.

Accusations in Campaigning

The study posed the question : "Politicians in media campaigns concentrate more on accusing each other. What response will it generate among the audience"? Without committing themselves on the audience response, most of them (38.14%) considered the practice as not ethical (Table No. 8.7). A little over one-fifth (22.68%) opined it generated disinterest while 19.58% said it generated controversy, but an equal percentage felt it generated interest which is perhaps noteworthy.

TABLE NO. 8.7 : **Distribution of Responses on the Effect of Political Accusations on the Minds of Audience (Q. No. 34)**

Party		*It generates interest*	*It generates controversy*	*It generates disinterest*	*It is not ethical*	*Total*
Congress (I)	Fre	10	9	10	20	49
	%	20.40	18.36	20.40	20	-
T.D.P.	Fre	3	7	7	7	24
	%	12.5	29.16	29.16	29.16	-
B.J.P.	Fre	3	-	3	4	10
	%	30	-	30	40	-
Communists	Fre	2	2	1	4	9
	%	22.22	22.22	11.11	44.44	-
Others	Fre	1	1	1	2	5
	%	20	20	20	40	-
Total	Fre	19	19	22	37	97
	%	19.58	19.58	22.68	38.14	-

A section of the party managers were of the opinion that unless a politician does that kind of a job of accusing, the audience do not get attracted to speech or broadcast (and tend to leave the place early) and hence they are forced to adopt such methods. Some expressed that if the members of other party deserve such kind of treatment, there is nothing wrong calling them liars. The overall response indicates the different stances chosen by the leaders on political bickering over media.

Much thought has been shed in the past on political accusations generating controversy. Blumler[9] recorded the following observations.

> "The mass media, by the way in which they structure and present political reality, may contribute to a widespread and chronic distrust of political life. Such distrust is not primarily a mark of sophistication, indicating that critical discount is at work. It is of a projective character and constitutes a defensive reaction against the

periodic political crisis known to affect a person's destiny as well as against what are defined as deliberate efforts to mobilize political sentiment".

As noted earlier majority of the sample felt accusing other parties and candidates in media campaigning as not ethical. The elders were slightly more concerned about this trend than the others.

Positionwise, more number of ministers thought that such accusations generate interest among the voters. This looks quite surprising as normally during campaigning it is the opposition groups who indulge in heavy criticism than the ruling ones. Being in responsible position normally ministers try to present a sober picture before the electorate. But this response shows they perhaps are under the impression that opposition parties draw the attention of voters through accusations and hence that could be a necessary evil in campaigning. However, it is observed by many that accusations are very common for both ruling and opposition parties with slight variations.

Empty Promises and Credibility of Radio and Television

Broadcast media claims more credibility compared to other media of mass communication. The sample's response was sought whether in their opinion the credibility of the media would be damaged in the long run if politicians are allowed to go on air with empty promises. 42% assessed the damage as 'to some extent' followed by 22% 'to great extent'. The number who felt in the opposite way was also quite sizeable (35%) (Table No 8.8). This group thinks that individual credibility of the person making empty promises is at stake but no damage is caused to the media because of this practice. But some expressed doubts even about Radio/TV's credibility in real sense. However the Communists could see some relationship between the two aspects.

TABLE NO. 8.8 : **Distribution of Responses as to What Extent Empty Promises would Damage the Credibility of Broadcasts Media (Q. No. 35)**

Party		*To a great extent*	*To some extent*	*Not at all*	*Don't know*	*Total*
Congress (I)	Fre	10	19	20	1	50
	%	20	38	40	2	-
T.D.P.	Fre	6	12	7	-	25
	%	24	48	28	-	-
B.J.P.	Fre	1	5	4	-	10
	%	10	50	40	-	-
Communists	Fre	4	4	2	-	10
	%	40	40	20	-	-
Others	Fre	1	2	2	-	5
	%	20	40	40	-	-
Total	Fre & %	22	42	35	1	100

Partywise, Communists estimated the damage to the media to be of great extent because of empty promises. Personal discussions revealed that they were not happy with the developing trends in the election campaigning, especially such as empty promises which have become the order of the day. This could be the reason for Communists' high consent in spite of their general criticism about media's partiality at times.

Agewise, elders' contribution to the majority opinion (to some extent) was more. They have further supported this by giving low score to the category 'not at all'. But positionwise more number of non-ministers disagreed with this argument.

Raising the Aspirations

The final question of this part is "Communication researchers have observed that media campaigning raises aspirations and when politicians fail to fulfil the promises it leads to frustration especially amongst the rural voters. Do you agree?" Only half of the sample (50.50%) agreed and the number went down progressively for disagreement (21.21%) and strong disagreement (14.14%) (Table No. 8.9).

TABLE NO. 8.9 : **Distribution of Responses as to whether the Nonfulfilment of Promises would lead to Frustration amongst Rural Voters (Q. No. 36).**

Party		*Strongly agree*	*Agree*	*Disagree*	*Strongly disagree*	*Don't know*	*Total*
Congress (I)	Fre	1	25	11	9	4	50
	%	2	50	22	18	8	-
T.D.P.	Fre	6	12	3	2	1	24
	%	25	50	12.5	8.33	4.16	-
B.J.P.	Fre	1	5	2	2	-	10
	%	10	50	20	20	-	-
Communists	Fre	1	4	4	1	-	10
	%	10	40	40	10	-	-
Others	Fre	-	4	1	-	-	5
	%	-	80	20	-	-	-
Total	Fre	9	50	21	14	5	99
	%	9.09	50.50	21.21	14.14	5.05	-

The leaders who disagreed with this observation thought the problem as a common factor for all kinds of campaigns and not for media alone. Partywise, TDP attached more weightage to this observation (75%) and Communists were equally divided between the two alternatives. Schramme[10] observes that "among rural masses media campaign raises aspirations and when the promises are not fulfilled frustration is caused". For example if electrification of all the villages by a certain period is promised over Radio and Television by a minister, hopes are raised among the rural folk (at least some) in spite of earlier disappointments. When the same is not implemented and the process gets repeated they might feel frustrated. While this supports the agreement of 50% of the respondents Cockerell[11] observes the problem from a different angle. To this extent he quotes Edward Heath the ex-British Prime Minister who once said in his election broadcast "I think perhaps sometimes too much is asked of politicians, too much is asked of Governments. It might also be the fault of politicians that they lead people to expect too much of them. Perhaps there ought to be a little more modesty and humility all around". Since the observation came from the heart of a politician this can be considered as the proper reason for the samples' low agreement to the statement under question.

TDP strongly agreed with this statement with a high score and gave less credit to "strongly disagree" on the scale compared to other parties. No specific reason could be thought for this deviation except that the leaders might have judged the statements based on their personal opinions than party philosophy.

The aged politicians' acceptance in this aspect seems partial since they did not attach any score to 'strongly agree' and also gave some score to 'strongly disagree' on the scale.

A few highly stimulating individual comments made during discussions on the questions of this part are reproduced below :

— TV giving publicity to less established contenders is only superficial.
— The problem of unsophistication of the politicians and voters is applicable only to live programmes.
— Accusing other parties in broadcasts is unethical but criticism of shortcomings is justified. However much depends upon whether the accusation is justified or is only slanderous. If justified it has the effect of exposing an undeserving candidate and serves the interest of democracy. On the contrary it will have a bad effect on the person who makes accusations, as also on the person against whom it was directed.

The following are the major conclusions of the present analysis.

For many politicians Radio and T.V. promote only passive learning among the electorates. They also differed on the issue of political parties accusing each other over media and its impact on the voters. While no partywise difference was observed in the above responses the same was noticed in the following.

Majority believe in Broadcast media's capability as domestic media in leading masses into active political participation. They also gave credit to this media for breaking barriers in reaching the remote voters. Regarding Radio/T.V. maintaining non-partisan stance in party conflict a ruling and opposition division was prominently observed among the respondents. The power of T.V. as a political medium in giving publicity to less established contenders was recognized by majority of the politicians. However they partially accepted the observation that the unsophistication of voters and politicians may pose difficulties in programme making over Radio/TV. Regarding empty promises of politicians causing damage to the credibility of the media—majority assessed the harm as to be significant while the number who thought opposite way was also quite sizeable. Many agreed that failure in implementing the election promises committed over media broadcasts leads to frustration amongst the rural masses.

While the influence of age was observed on the responses position as a variable did not show much impact except in a few areas.

The discussion can be wound up with a broad note on the representatives' co-operation in answering the questions especially in the present part. The leaders in general appeared to give reasonable consideration to the observations and findings of political communication research whatever they happened to know. Some of them applied much thought and analysed the authenticity of these findings in the light of the present conditions. While accepting the factual aspects they were shrewd in denying what they did not believe. It is interesting that many apparently have not allowed their party ideology to influence their responses and judged the statements purely with individual objectivity and rationality. The responses can be claimed as authentic since most of them are mature, responsible and thoughtful citizens. The contradictions in the statements are very negligible keeping in view the limited scope of the present party broadcasts. However most of the observations in this part have been covered by media researchers and some information is common knowledge. There is also a possibility that the respondents might have agreed to the observations half-heartedly (avoiding the risk of refuting them altogether) since they are the conclusions of research done by political scientists and media researchers. Nonetheless the sample's response to this part of the study may serve as some background to programme production.

REFERENCES

1. Gamble, Michael W., and Gamble, Teri Kwal; *Introducing Mass Communication* : Singapore, McGraw Hill Book Company 1989, p. 453.
2. Blumler J.G., *The Political Effects of Mass-communication*, The Audience Unit—8, The Open University Social Sciences, a third level course, Milton Keyness, Walton Hal, p. 46.
3. Barwise, Patrick and Ehrenberg, Andrew; *Television and its Audience*; London, Sage Publications Ltd., 1988, p. 123.
4. Cockerell, Michael : Live from No. 10—*The inside story of Prime Ministers and Television*, London, Faber and Faber Ltd. 1988.
5. Tyrrel, Robert : *The Work of the Television Journalist*, London. Focal Press, pp. 153 and 154.
6. Cockerell, Michael; *op. cit.*, p. 168.

7. Boyd, Andrew; *Broadcast Journalism—Techniques of Radio and T.V. News;* Oxford, Heinmann Professional Publishing Ltd.
8. Pilsworth, Michael; set T.V. free and let the people see Crewe, Ivor and Harrop, Martin; Ed.; *Political Communications,* The general election campaign of 1983, Cambridge; Cambridge University Press, 1986, p. 310 and 311.
9. Blumler, J.G; *op. cit.,* p. 37.
10. Schramme, Wilbur; *Mass-media and National Development,* California, Stanford University Press, 1964.
11. Cockerell, Michael; *op. cit.,* p. 212.

Chapter 9

POLITICAL ATTITUDES : EFFECTS OF MEDIA

After analyzing the responses of the politicians about the existing set-up, nature and scope of various media units, knowledge about the target group, improvements in the present set-up and the perceived image of the media, the present part deals with two major aspects concerning election broadcasts. Eventhough no miracles can be expected in the near future under the present conditions a comparative look into the status of PBs in the past, present and future may provide some ideas for effective programming. Secondly, the main focus of present political communication research is on the "effects of media campaigning and voting behaviour" especially in influencing the attitudes. Knowledge about the factors which influence the voters and the voting pattern is a pre-requisite for assessing the political impact of Radio/TV on voters. Meaningful conclusions cannot be drawn from any study unless the related factors are given the due consideration. For this purpose the study explored the imagination of the representatives with the help of a few questions.

Political Attitudes—Effects of Media

Three questions were put to the sample at different times during the interview (i.e. in different parts of the questionnaire) to know their opinions about the impact of party broadcasts in the past, present and future. A comparative look into the responses revealed a progressive change from negative response to positive from the past to future (Graph No. 9.1). The responses are discussed in detail below.

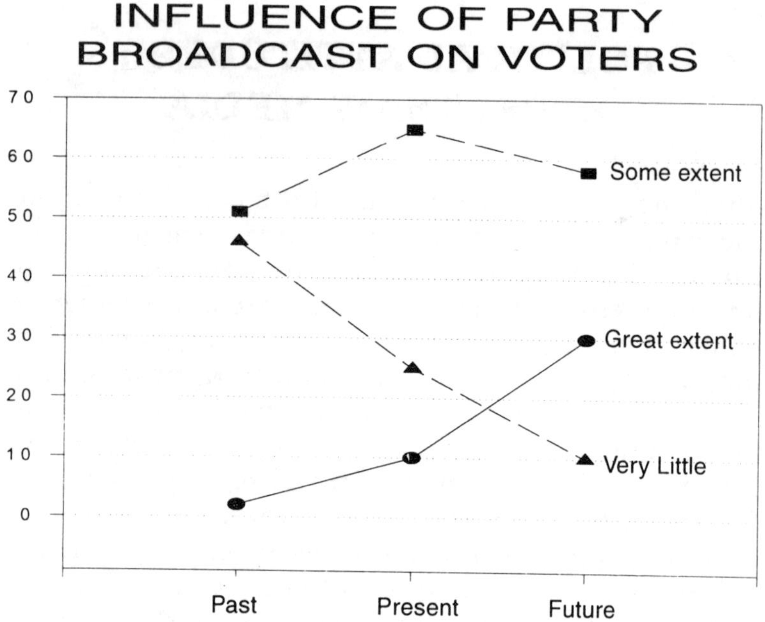

Graph No. 9.1

Influence of Party Broadcasts in the Past

The political leaders were not quite satisfied with the influence of pre-election Broadcasts on voters in the past and many of them felt that it was only to some extent (51% of Them) or very little (46% of them) (See table No. 9.1). Comparisons across the parties revealed that Congress (I) was the most dissatisfied with a high score to the 'very little' category (56%).

General Impact of Party Broadcasts on Voters

A question intended to know whether they have any confidence in party broadcasts in general was put to the sample. 65% assessed the influence as only 'to

TABLE NO. 9.1 : **Distribution of Responses on the Influence of Pre-election Broadcasts on the Voters in the Past (Q. No. 2)**

Party		*To a great extent*	*To some extent*	*Very little*	*Not at all*	*Total*
Congress (I)	Fre	1	10	28	1	50
	%	2	40	56	2	-
T.D.P.	Fre	1	15	9	-	25
	%	4	60	36	-	-
B.J.P.	Fre	-	6	4	-	10
	%	-	60	40	-	-
Communists	Fre	-	8	2	-	10
	%	-	80	20	-	-
Others	Fre	-	2	3	-	5
	%	-	40	60	-	-
Total	Fre & %	2	51	46	1	100

some extent' 25% to 'very little' and only 10% 'to a great extent' (Table No. 9.2). Similar view was expressed regarding the influence of these broadcasts in the past also probably due to the effect of past performance of Radio and TV. Though the group accepted the potentiality of the media the responses gave an impression that they were not optimistic in achieving their goals through Radio and TV.

The middle aged politicians felt that the impact of pre-election broadcasts on audience in general would be to a great extent. Since this group is more active in politics they must have experienced the need for media campaigning in the field as compared to youngsters (mostly MLAs and Party workers) and elders.

While ministers thought the effect to be of great extent, the other group assessed as very little impact. The general opinion that Radio/TV are misused for ruling party's publicity could be the reason for ministers viewing this aspect positively and non-ministers negatively.

TABLE NO. 9.2 : **Distribution of Responses on the Impact of Pre-Election Broadcasts on the Audience (Q. No. 16)**

Party		*To a great extent*	*To some extent*	*Very little*	*Not at all*	*Total*
Congress (I)	Fre	6	26	18	-	50
	%	12	52	36	-	-
T.D.P.	Fre	3	18	4	-	25
	%	12	72	16	-	-
B.J.P.	Fre	1	8	1	-	10
	%	10	80	10	-	-
Communists	Fre	-	9	1	-	10
	%	-	90	10	-	-
Others	Fre	-	4	1	-	5
	%	-	80	20	-	-
Total	Fre & %	10	65	25	-	100

Effect of PBs in Future

When asked how they visualise the effect, 58% rated it only 'to some extent'. This was followed by 'to a great extent' (30%) and 'very little' (10%) (Table No. 9.3). The group who carried high hopes related the effect to increase in the quantity and quality of the party broadcasts and awareness about media campaigning among the voters. Provided these two conditions, party broadcasts will certainly have a greater impact—they opined.

While elders rating it 'not to a great extent' sounds reasonable, youngsters feeling the effect 'to be very little' (relatively) is not on expected lines. May be they also opine that Radio/TV influence the voters only superficially and not deeply. The disappointment caused by the present broadcasts also seems to be one of the factors that is standing in the way of estimating the effect of the media in future by the respondents. Position-wise a small group among non-ministers thought the effect to be 'very little' as compared to ministers.

TABLE NO. 9.3 : **Distribution of Responses on the Influence of Radio/TV on the most Deep-seated Political Attitudes of the Voters in Future (Q. No. 40)**

Party		*To a great extent*	*To some extent*	*Very little*	*Not at all*	*Total*
Congress I	Fre	13	28	7	2	50
	%	26	56	14	4	-
T.D.P.	Fre	13	11	1	-	25
	%	52	44	4	-	-
B.J.P.	Fre	2	7	1	-	10
	%	20	70	10	-	-
Communist	Fre	2	7	1	-	10
	%	20	70	10	-	-
Others	Fre	-	5	-	-	5
	%	-	100	-	-	-
Total	Fre & %	30	58	10	2 .	100

Research on the impact of party broadcasts in influencing the deep-seated political attitudes of voters is still undergoing experimentation. Though invasion of television has eradicated the earlier doubts, researchers are still engaged in studying the role of social and psychological factors in decision making process.

An examination of different trends in political communication research may well describe how the deep-seated political attitudes of the voters are influenced by the media. Earlier, political communication research has mostly concentrated on persuasion i.e., the association between communication and attitudes concerning voting decisions. But now some changes are noticed in the methodology. The basis for the change seems to be certain doubts about—mass-media especially newspapers, Radio and Television that they only transmit information and do not make efforts for persuasion. The feedback mechanisms of the above media also do not really undertake persuasion studies. This has necessitated the researchers to shift their attention towards audience in assessing the impact of the media. How does the information transmitted influence the attitudes of the voters? What are the observations of researchers in this regard? Blumler[1] says "The crucial conceptual distinction that has arisen through many studies is between attitudes and cognitions". To this effect he quotes Becker, McCombs and McLeod (1975) who defined these terms as :

> "Attitudes are summary evaluations of objects by individuals : cognitions are stored information about these objects held by individuals. Evaluations may be based on cognitions and that dynamics of the relationship between the two may be complex. Nevertheless, cognitions can be measured independently of attitudes and can be assessed against some external objective criterion of communicated information."

The media effects model by Becker *et al.* (1975) clearly shows the two phases of political communication research. While the first phase represents the cognitive effects research the second attitude change.

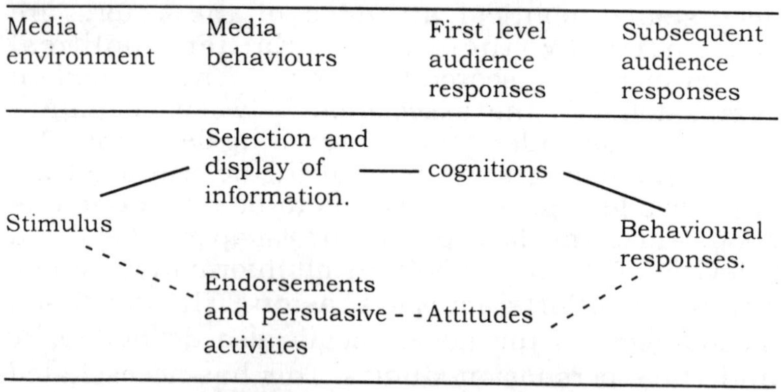

Figure : Media effects model
Source : Blumler—media effects research[2]

Blumler[3] observes many present day researchers to be having interest in cognitive effects of exposure to mass-media materials. To this effect he quotes Wade (1973) who has referred to the ability of the media to create images of social realities by which the public may structure their views of the world and Kraus and Davis (1976) who maintain that in many crucial and diverse ways the mass media create reality, defining activities and events, moulding and shaping a variety of images for us. Thus Blumler concludes more stress is now being placed on how the media project definitions of the situations that political actors must cope with, than on attitudes towards those actors themselves.

Factors Influencing the Voters

Many factors play an important role during elections in influencing the voters. Three factors however stand out as major ones. They are the party, the candidate and the publicity. The influence of these factors depends on the type of political system a country adopts. While parties occupy important place in one system, candidates exercise more influence in other. Sometimes publicity dominates the other two factors. Discussing the situation in Britain, Harrop[4] says "British elections are more often about competence than policies. They are about the parties' abilities to achieve common objectives (high employment, low inflation, real economic growth), not the objectives themselves. They are about the parties' capacity to govern their unity, their direction, their implementation skills. Because competence is a managerial rather than a philosophical characteristic, perceptions of a party's ability can change over time and thus help to account for electoral change.

In the present study each factor was dealt separately in detail to know the opinions of the leaders.

1. Party

Party performance in the past, followed by party policies, programmes and manifesto were considered as important factors in influencing the voters (Table No 9.4). However, BJP gave first preference to the latter. On the whole there is not much difference between the alternative responses. The respondents' preference supports the observation of political scientists made earlier in this aspect. As observed by Harrop[5], Butler and Stokes (1960) suggested that "most voters did not think or vote in ideological terms. They had almost a nominal understanding of terms such as 'left' and 'right' and did not organise their attitudes to policies in a way that suggested any clear structure. Parties, not principles, were the lenses through which voters viewed politics". This perspective has been disputed by several recent writers. For example Himmelweit *et al* (1983) suggest that political ideology is an increasingly important feature of electors' political evaluations, underpinning their attitudes to specific issues. Heath *et al* (1983) believe that voters form an overall perception of what the parties stand for and these perceptions can be regarded as 'ideological interpretations of politics by voters.

Harrop feels these definitions do not capture the abstract nature of an ideology and Butler and Stoke's contention that most voters do not think ideologically still may stand in the present context. However, he opines that there is some weak structure as to how voters think about politics.

Agewise analysis brought out some difference of opinion in this aspect even though less significant. Seniors slightly gave more score to party performance

TABLE NO. 9.4 : **Distribution of Factors influencing the Voter's Party (Q. No. 12)**

(a) Party

Party		*Party policies, progra-mme and manifesto*	*Party perfor-mance in the past*	*Caliber of leader in a party*	*Party organi-zation and cadre*	*Party Symbol*
Con-	% responded	92	2	82	52	30
gress (I)	Mean score	1.89	1.51	2.51	3.15	4
T.D.P.	% responded	96	88	84	80	40
	Mean score	2.12	1.95	2.19	3	4.8
B.J.P.	% responded	100	90	70	90	30
	Mean score	1.8	2	2.85	2.44	5
Com-	% responded	80	80	60	90	10
munists	Mean score	2.5	2.22	3.16	2.77	5
Others	% responded	80	80	80	40	20
	Mean score	1.75	1.75	2.75	2	1

in the past as an influencing factor on voters. But youngsters (Group I) relatively rated party organisation and cadre as more influential. Middle aged sample attached marginally more score to party symbol compared to others. The preferences clearly speak out the influence of age in this area. Middle aged members suggesting publicity to party symbol reflect their practical approach in assessing the advantage of such facility during election time.

As regards the influence of position, "Party performance in the past" was claimed as an influencing factor by non-ministers. Since opposition is generally critical of the ruling party, they might have felt that bad performance of a party will have much impact on the voters' mind during elections. It is also normally observed that people who are not aware of the practical difficulties of being a minister tend to think in ideal terms about the task and will be under illusion of forming a better government than the existing one. However, the fact that this factor (bad performance) has changed the fate of many parties in the past cannot be ignored here. An interesting point to note is that parties were given the chance to form the government in the past either independently or in alliance with others, but most of the times the performance of these parties has led the country to another election exercise. In the recent times this type of behaviour of the voters was termed as 'desire for change'. Voters' dissatisfaction over a ruling party's performance and the experimental attitude of voters in giving an opportunity to the other alternatives to see how far the new party stands up to their expectations were also observed as the potential reasons behind voters political intentions by many political scientists. One such observation of electoral behaviour by Dunleavy[6] is :

> "Voters in political markets behave as rational actors rather like consumers in economic markets, by choosing the party programme closest to their own views on important issues. They maximise the benefits they receive from party programmes after allowing for any costs. Key issues normally include inflation, unemployment and income growth, since people are basically self-interested. Some voters with clear-cut economic interests are consistently better off under one party than with its rivals, and develop brand loyalty. But this attachment is always reconsidered if a better alternate appears or 'the brand' gives declining satisfaction. Voters discount infeasible promises, however, and treat manifesto pledges sceptically. Instead of assessing conflicting promises about the future, they can decide to reward or punish the incumbent government for its performance, basing their judgements mainly on short term economic variables. So a prosperous election year can make up for harder times in the past."

Candidate

Candidate's performance in the past and their honesty and integrity were given more marks by all the respondents (Table No. 9.5) Cong(I) attached first preference to honesty and integrity of the candidate and the other three parties considered "candidate's performance in the past as the most important factor in influencing the voters." However the difference in figures is not of much significance. During discussion majority of the sample opined that candidate's educational qualification play very little role as a deciding factor in winning elections. An educated person without honesty or integrity is of no use to the party. They expressed their genuine indignation that unfortunately caste, money power and muscle power are dominating the present day election scene. Explaining the role of party leaders in influencing the voters Dunleavy[7] says : "Party leaders are rational actors, who maximize votes in the electoral market, rather as businessmen maximize profits in economic markets".

TABLE NO. 9.5 : **Distribution of Factors influencing the Voters (Q. No. 12)**

(b) *Candidate*

Party		*Education*	*Religion*	*Performance in the past*	*Caste*	*Honesty/ integrity*
Congress (I)	% responded	50	22	94	38	82
	Mean score	2.92	3.36	1.80	2.36	1.73
T.D.P.	% responded	60	36	92	48	84
	Mean score	3.2	3.44	1.65	2.58	2.33
B.J.P.	% responded	40	10	90	60	100
	Mean score	2.75	3	1.55	3	1.7
Communists	% responded	30	20	90	40	90
	Mean score	3	4	1.33	2.75	2.22
Others	% responded	20	-	80	40	100
	Mean score	3	-	1.5	1.5	2

While elders seem to have considered religion of the candidate as a more important influencing factor on voters, youngsters relatively attached a little higher score to education, honesty and integrity. However the difference is of less significance. Positionwise education was given slightly higher score by the ministers.

In general educational qualification of a candidate was not felt so important by a majority. They were uncompromising in pointing out the disadvantages of electing an educated person without any integrity. However ministers might have thought that being in the government and holding responsible positions they ought to promote certain values irrespective of their influence on voters. The sample's response in this respect is quite thought-provoking. The party managers rated honesty and integrity of the candidates as an important factor in influencing the voters and offered low score to education. They also think that an educated man without honesty and integrity will be of no use. While the respect shown to honesty and integrity is appreciable the low concern for education once again highlights the prevailing misconceptions about education in general. Education *per se* should promote honesty and integrity. The feedback which looks these two in isolation raises the question whether the fault lies with education or people.

Publicity

In this study, the politicians viewed that the important factors influencing the voters are public meetings followed by media propaganda (Table No. 9.6). However, most of them rated door-to-door campaign, if it could be conducted, as the most effective mode, especially in rural areas. Door-to-door campaign was rated high by the below 45 age group. In case of party symbol as an influencing factor considerable difference in mean scores was observed between the two groups i.e. ministers and non-ministers. Ministers attached more importance to the symbol in party broadcasts. Similarly ministers gave a little higher score to public meetings as an influential medium during elections to reach the voters than the other group.

TABLE NO. 9.6 : **Distribution of Factors Influencing the Voters (Q. No. 12)**

(c) *Publicity*

Party		*Media propa-ganda*	*Media adver-tise-ment*	*Public meet-ings*	*Any other pl sp-ecify*	*Door to door campaign*
Con	% responded	62	44	80	16	30
gresss (I)	Mean score	1.93	2.68	1.42	1.37	1.46
T.D.P.	% responded	60	40	68	20	28
	Mean score	1.88	2.6	1.52	2.6	1.57
B.J.P.	% responded	80	20	70	20	-
	Mean score	1.75	2	1.28	2.5	-
Com-	% responded	50	10	70	30	-
munists	Mean score	1.2	3	1.85	1.66	-
Others	% responded	80	40	100	-	-
	Mean score	1.5	3	1.4	-	-

Voting Pattern

In a democracy voters have the last word. As such the entire election mechanism of parties, especially campaigning, is geared to the final stage i.e., voting. What determines the voting pattern of a voter? There are many factors-intelligence of voters, commitment to the party, desire for change etc., and it is not always that leaders are able to assess these factors correctly and design strategies before getting into the field. During personal interviews the researcher herself could observe the mounting tension among the leaders when they received information about how the other party is playing the game and what new methods have to be adopted to counteract. It is common knowledge that any new issue that crops up during elections is fully exploited by all political parties to their best advantage although they may not attach any significance to the same issue during other times.

To a question which, in order to rating, determine the voting pattern of a voter (among six alternatives) the sample rated 'commitment' first followed by "along the wave" (Table No. 9.7). The difference between the two was not much. 'Propaganda effect' secured only the third place. Some people said that each factor will have its own effect at different times. For a few all factors work together. Some felt it difficult to predict and opined that no one knows till the opening of the ballot box how best they may try to guess the outcome. Public opinion polls and field surveys for this purpose serve only human interest, they explained. According to some, voters are very intelligent and have been teaching lessons to leaders and parties in every election.

The fact that party broadcasts falling under propaganda effect secured only a third place in rating, reflect their low profile in the present electioneering process. Partywise BJP gave first preference to "along the wave" followed by "intuition". The other three parties held more or less similar opinions. The varied responses of the leaders necessitate further analysis. "Along the wave" which secured the second highest score may need another look here. "Wave" is not just a freak mass-behaviour. It emerges as a collective decision to oppose or to support a particular ideology or issues that prevailed. Waves have indeed made considerable impact on elections of the recent past. This perhaps might have led the sample giving preference to 'wave'. BJP which depends on the

TABLE NO. 9.7 : **Distribution of Factors determining the Voting Pattern (Q. No. 22)**

Party		*Intelligence*	*Commitment*	*Along the wave*	*Intuition*	*Propaganda effect*	*Inducements in cash or kind*
Congress (I)	% responded	32	68	74	26	60	42
	Mean score	3.93	1.73	1.97	4.38	2.9	3.09
T.D.P.	% responded	32	72	80	16	56	52
	Mean score	4.25	1.61	1.8	4.75	2.5	3.23
B.J.P.	% responded	50	40	90	50	60	40
	Mean score	4.22	2.75	1.77	2.2	2.83	4.25
Communists	% responded	30	70	50	20	50	20
	Mean score	2.66	1	1.8	3.5	2.8	4
Others	% responded	20	40	100	20	60	40
	Mean score	4	2	1	3	2.2	4

strength of the cadre base also seems to submit to this 'wave' as the first ranking factor. "Propaganda effect" in which media plays a major role securing only a third place also calls for reflection. While one can understand the politicians' preference for commitment, their helplessness against 'wave' seems to push the propaganda effect to a third place. However, from the media point of view, one can perhaps observe an indirect role of mass media in creating 'wave' during elections. Wave is a rebellious or determined response to certain problems or issues under debate. In presenting these issues before the electorate, analysing and influencing or provoking, media plays a crucial and major role. Hence, it can be said that media have both direct and indirect contribution in campaigning. However, one cannot deny the fact that "wave" is usually talked of when people opt for a big change.

More youngsters compared to the middle aged marked 'intuition'. Similarly they outnumbered the other two in supporting propaganda effect as a deciding factor of the voting pattern. Inducements in cash or kind were not given much importance. However ministers gave a little higher score to this.

According to one experienced politician, the factors that influence the voting pattern differ with the nature of election. In the local elections to municipalities etc., inducements in cash or kind may work, whereas in the parliamentary elections it is probably a wave that plays the role-commented.

Do Politicians Listen/Watch their Rivals

The main objective of the last question of the study is to know the level of the politicians' exposure to the party broadcasts. The questionnaire had to be administered before the announcement of the election results as party broadcasts are completed just before elections. Due to the obvious difficulties in administering the questionnaire on persons who were busy with hectic campaigning the mode of question was changed. The leaders were asked whether they plan to listen to/watch the broadcasts of political parties other than their own. A large number (94%) said 'yes' and partywise also the same opinion was seen. BJP was particularly unanimous (Table No 9.8). Lack of time was claimed as the sole reason for not listening to/watching these programmes. Among the six who said they had no such plan to listen to/watch the other party broadcasts some felt that unless the other partyman was a good orator or an extraordinary speaker it would be a sheer waste to watch. The representatives who listen to/watch the broadcast of other parties felt that it would give them an opportunity in knowing the views of the other parties.

TABLE NO. 9.8 : **Distribution of Responses whether the Politicians Listen to/Watch to the Other Party Broadcasts (Q. No. 41)**

Party		*Yes*	*No*	*Total*
Congress (I)	Fre	48	2	50
	%	96	4	-
T.D.P.	Fre	24	1	25
	%	96	4	-
B.J.P.	Fre	10	-	10
	%	100	-	-
Communists	Fre	8	2	10
	%	80	20	-
Others	Fre	4	1	5
	%	80	20	-
Total	Fre & %	94	6	100

The following are the major conclusions of the present analysis :

As regards the impact of election broadcast on voters, a comparative look into the data revealed progressive change from negative responses to positive from the past to the future. Party performance in the past followed by party policies, programmes and manifesto were considered as contributing factors in influencing the voters. Candidate's performance in the past, clubbed with honesty and integrity, were preferred more by all the respondents. Politicians viewed that the important factors influencing the voters are public meetings followed by media propaganda. Door-to-door campaign was also considered as an effective medium if it could be properly conducted.

'Commitment' followed by 'along the wave' were claimed as the determinants of the voting pattern of a voter. Propaganda effect secured a poor third place. However, the sample differed partywise. To some extent age and position have shown influence on the responses. Majority of the politicians plan to listen to/watch PBs if time permits.

REFERENCES

1. Blumler, Jay G.; The Political Effects of Mass Communications, The Audience Unit. The Open University Social Sciences a third level course, Milton Keyness, Walton Hall, p. 23.
2. *Ibid.,* p. 24.
3. *Ibid.,* p. 24.
4. Harrop Martin; *Voting and the Electorate.* Drucker, Henry *et al; Developments in British Politics,* London, MacMillan Education Ltd, 1983, p. 51.
5. *Ibid.,* p. 47 & 48.
6. Dunleavy Patrick; *Topics in British Politics—Electoral Behaviour,* Drucker, Henry *et al., op. cit.,* p. 338 & 339.
7. *Ibid.,* p. 342.

Chapter 10

MEDIA COVERAGE OF ELECTIONS

(Voting models and agenda setting approaches)

The relationship between media campaigning and voting behaviour has been the main focus of research in the field of political communication. Various models have been suggested to account for voting behaviour and media coverage. Do these models have any relevance in the present context? The preceding chapters have analysed the perceptions of politicians of Andhra Pradesh pertaining to the role of Radio and Television in party politics. Now, it is proposed to relate these perceptions to the available research models. In particular Harrop's voting models and the agenda setting theory of media (widely accepted by many) have been examined for this purpose. Which model do the Andhra Pradesh politicians seem to conform to/fit into? Are there partywise differences too? Or could an altogether new model be fit to their perceptions/responses?

Models of Voting

Harrop[1] indentified three models of voting behaviour. (1) Party identification model, (2) The radical model, and (3) The issue voting model. The first model stresses the importance of family socialization as a mechanism linking social cleavages to individual choice. It also suggests that party identification is passed on from parents to children along with other loyalties. Partisanship strengthens with age, sustained by interaction with people of similar views, as electors come to rely on their allegiance to solve the problem of interpreting complex political information. The radical model believes that people vote in accordance with their social interests, though political parties and the mass-media both influence the interpretation of these interests. The focus of this model is on the complex patterns of interests in society, rather than on the individual elector. It is a sociological rather than a socio/psychological approach. The 'issue voting model' threats the voter as an informed consumer, choosing between parties on the basis of which comes closest to or is least distant from the voters own conceptions of what governments should do. This model sees voters acting individually and not collectively or expressively. The broad concept of issues can be divided into three Parts—Party's ideology, party's specific policies and party's competence.

Now if we examine the responses of the sample to the question, "which in their opinion determines the voting pattern of a voter", the politicians rated "commitment" followed by "along the wave" as the important factors. Does this response satisfy any of Harrop's models of voting?

If we try to fit our politicians' opinion into the first model, the importance given to "commitment" cannot be attributed to party identification model completely even though party royalty is a part of family socialization which may influence the individual choice. In general this model was found to be weak by political scientists. And also in the Indian context, commitment in politics has a broader definition than just royalty to family. Commitment to a particular party can be due to various other reasons. Initially a person may sympathize with a particular party as a part of family socialization but the 'royalty' factor may not guide him as he becomes mature. As it happens in many cases, he will try to adjust his behaviour according to the interests of the society rising above the family royalty. If the party ideology does not eventually fit to his perceptions there is a possible shift in his opinion. Hence it can be concluded that the party identification model does not cover the commitment aspect of our leaders perception of voting behaviour. Unfortunately the questionnaire does not provide further scope and information to test this model.

The sample's preference does not satisfy the requirements of issue voting model also as it expects the voter to be well informed and individualistic. Harrop divides issues into three categories—party's ideology, party's specific policies and party's competence. The questionnaire sought the responses of all leaders on these issues in detail. They gave preference to all the three aspects as important factors in influencing the voters. However party's competence (party's performance in the past) was rated slightly higher than others. BJP gave first preference to party policies, programmes and manifesto. While this response speaks of the influence in general, the issue voting model expects the voter to be well informed and to be able to take a decision after analysing the parties ideology, policies and programmes and competence. Is this situation obtaining now? It is common knowledge that most of our voters are illiterate or not well educated to discuss the issues and their understanding of politics is probably very limited. They usually do not give the impression of having detailed knowledge about the political parties whether the parties are fighting on any issue if so the specifications. Thus the leaders' perceptions of "commitment" and "along the wave" on the voting pattern seem to clearly reject the issue voting model.

The Radical model speaks of the social interests of the people. Though this model is not as distant as the above two from Indian context, it also does not fulfil the requirements. While commitment has some relevance to radical model, wave negates this theory. Though wave is usually considered as a rebellious response to the changing patterns of social interests, by nature it is an emotional upsurge which need not always be based on a radical philosophy.

While the three models do not satisfy the Indian conditions the responses can perhaps be fit into an altogether different framework which may explain the average Indian voter's behaviour to some extent. Commitment and wave have a limited role in representing party royalty, understanding of issues and social interests, but an emotional response can occur under both situations. While emotionalism is an inherent characteristic of commitment, "wave" occurs generally under conditions like charisma, sentiment or sympathy and emotional reaction to certain issues. One can see the increasing influence of these characteristics in the recent elections. Parties develop or choose strategies based on these factors and depending on the moods of the electorate. This trend may occasionally represent social interests but mostly it is the emotional behaviour or upsurge that is observed in the voters' behaviour especially among the masses. However emotional model should not be understood as a mere reflection of an intuitive behaviour of voters during elections. It is the sum total of their assessment of the political situation prevailing at a particular time mostly guided by the emotions. The emotional theory speculates on the unpredictive and complex patterns of voting behaviour in a society under the influence of certain factors of mass appeal like charisma and sentiment. While this model cannot be claimed to represent any healthy trend, its existence and applicability have to be accepted and there is certainly a need to educate the masses in political affairs. The media have to play an effective role in achieving this task.

Coming back to Harrop's models of voting, let us examine how he relates the role of media to his models of voting. According to Harrop[2] the mass media play a major role in the radical model of voting. Television and the press are believed to define what are to count as acceptable political views, to influence citizens into similar modes of thinking and also to create a stream of messages which can favour one particular party. By contrast, the party identification model views the media as just a reinforcing influence on voting decisions, providing material which is selectively interpreted by voters whose standing commitment to a party insulates them from the effects of the media. In the issue voting model, the media are seen more as a source of information than values. The reinforcement interpretation of the media is no longer an adequate guide to media effects. Here the party identification model is rather weak.

The role of media as defined by Harrop is not exactly the same in the Indian context at present. As discussed in the preceding chapters, illiteracy, non-availability of television sets, inadequate political programming and the limitations of official media restrict the scope of media influence, especially in playing an intended role. In the emotional model also, media play a big role but ironically through programmes that are not necessarily intended for electoral purposes. Even if the official media cater to the information needs and can have only subtle effect on emotions, private media can work up emotions more manifestly. The advent of cable television and other private channels may further strengthen the emotional angle in influencing the voting behaviour. However as Harrop[3] rightly observes, the media can be considered as having influence on voting behaviour in four situations. That is when : (1) party loyalties are weak, (2) there are new subjects to cover, (3) coverage is credible and (4) People rarely discuss politics. Television is accorded a special role as it has strengthened the credibility of the media and supplanted conversation as a major channel of political communication.

"Agenda setting" has been widely accepted as one of the important features of media coverage of politics. It sets a format and guiding principles for the priorities in media coverage of the electoral process and in influencing the voters. In addition to many aspects, one of the important points on which elections are fought are the "issues" which decide the fate of citizens. Issues are the most crucial matters for both political parties and electorate. Voters are expected to understand, analyse and decide the key issues of the time, observe the stances each party takes on different issues and decide their vote. Media's role is to inform and educate the electorate on these matters. In the Indian context this is being done broadly through programmes like news, focus, current affairs etc. The role of Radio/Television in highlighting and promoting discussion about the issues during elections has drawn the attention of many researchers. From these studies has emerged the role of "Agenda setting" by the media. Programmes broadcast during elections normally contain issues that are to concern to the electorate. There is enough scope for media to emotionalise the issues and for justifiable reasons. While transmitting these programmes, consciously or unconsciously media becomes a powerful instrument in the election mechanism. While many of the respondents appreciated this but some criticism surfaced. Past research also reveals the characteristics of this role.

Agenda setting election campaign programmes by Television is a complex and delicate subject. Sometimes producers' intervention in the election broadcasts are resented as infringement of the privilege of the politician. There is also a possibility of media people highlighting unimportant issues and setting a narrow agenda. The process can be discussed in two stages: the media—political parties' relations and the media-audience relations. In the latter, the broadcasters usually know the needs of the audience and prepare programmes accordingly. But in the former, problems arise in formulating an agenda itself. This is an interactive process requiring perfect coordination. While political parties give more importance to content, broadcasters are concerned about the technique and the customers' (audience) satisfaction about the programme. These interests may sometimes clash and lead to conflict.

Supporting these complexities, Blumler *et al.*,[4] explain four approaches to election agenda setting. They are : (1) prudential, (2) reactive, (3) conventionally journalistic and (4) analytical. These categories represent the way of sorting out the different approaches to election news-making. However they have a limitation in terms of choice and orientation. Each approach seems to point to a different set of interests as noted below.

Agenda Setting Orientation		*Main Points of Reference/Interest*
Prudential	-	The organisation
Reactive	-	Politicians as sources
Conventionally journalistic	-	Occupational values
Analytical	-	The public interest

Blumler *et al.*, summarize their observations as follows.

> "How newsmen strive to project an election campaign is not just a matter for internal debate. Their choices and decisions have important

consequences for all who depend on their coverage of major political events. First, the various approaches to journalistic agenda-setting may trigger or constrain different electioneering tactics. Prudential attitudes may encourage parties to develop calculated strategies of sharply angled complaints. A reactive philosophy could favour close collaboration between party managers and campaign reporters and a sign-posting of the party's intended message of the day (or hour) to their mutual convenience. The conventionally journalistic approach seems to invite a propaganda of nuggets, nutshells and golden phrases, including the staging where possible, of dramatic, combative and visually arresting incidents and accusations. The analytical approach, however, would presumably require politicians to elaborate their more substantive issues and policy positions".

Coming to the Indian context while private media are still at the beginning, the Government controlled media are not aggressive in political broadcasts. Hence, the suitability of these approaches to our context is doubtful. Only recently, the agenda-setting role of media is being discussed by a few broadcasters, that too audience research personnel in Radio and Television stations. However with the entry of foreign media and the growth of mass communications as an area of specialisation, there may be much scope for research on the topics like "different style of coverage of elections" etc. At present the role of press is more active in agenda setting than that of the electronic media. Radio/TV also give sufficient coverage during elections, but the programmes do not actually reflect the above four approaches. In general, the agenda setting of the press seems to be nearer to prudential and reactive approaches and the Radio/TV are perhaps closer to analytical approach. The conventionally journalistic approach is also not uncommon in the absence of definite policy guidelines.

A specific look into the representatives responses in the present study and the relevance of the above approaches may be of some interest here. The sample rated door-to-door campaign and public meetings as the most influential modes of campaigning during elections provided they can be implemented. Since they were sceptical about the possibility of implementing this, considerable weightage was given to press followed by TV as the influential media during elections. This clearly speaks of the conditions prevailing and the need to adopt a suitable approach to media-election campaigning. However the majority responses in favour of analytical programmes show the preference for analytical approach to media coverage of elections. The conventionally journalistic approach may create distrust among the audience. It may be recalled that a significant group felt that accusations in campaigning may create controversy and distrust. How do the media under the journalistic approach encourage such distrust? Who is more prone to it and how is it counteracted? Blumler[4] answers these questions with the help of a study conducted by Robinson (1976) who suspected that certain features of TV news reporting could have been responsible for the sharp decline of popular trust in government in the United States at that time. To this extent he quotes Robinson, who said :

> "My recent work with TV has forced me to build a yet untested theory concerning the growth of political illegitimacy. I have begun to envision a two-stage process in which TV journalism, with its constant emphasis on social and political conflict, its high credibility, its powerful

> audiovisual capabilities and its epidemicity, has caused the more vulnerable viewers first to doubt their own understanding of their political system. But once these individuals have passed this initial stage they enter a second phase in which personal denigration continues and in which a new hostility towards politics and government also emerges. Having passed through both stages of political cynicism, these uniquely suspectable individuals pass their cynicisms along with those who were, at the start, less attuned to TV messages and consequently less directly vulnerable to TV malaise".

Blumler further observed that to test the validity of this diagnosis, Robinson re-analysed the data secured during a nation-wide survey of American voters interviewed at the time of Presidential election campaign of 1968. He could prove his hypothesis to a maximum extent. However the methodological foundations of his study were subsequently attacked by Miller, Erbring and Goldenberg (1976).

What is the relationship between election agenda-media coverage and voting behaviour in Indian conditions? This is an area open for the political and media researchers to explore and find out the approaches that are helpful in setting agenda for media coverage of elections to influence the voting pattern of Indian electorate.

Agenda setting by media contributes to the emotional model of voting behaviour too. While it should cater to the requirements of "issue voting model" there is a possibility of influencing voting intentions of the electorate by projecting issues of emotional importance especially by the private media. In Government controlled media also the coverage of certain aspects in nonpolitical programmes may arouse emotional feelings. The above discussed four approaches also do this to a large extent but not exactly reflect the characteristics of a model that speaks an average Indian voting behaviour i.e., charisma, wave, sentiment etc.

Why politicians and journalists take the help of the above factors in achieving their goals? Obviously to "impress" the voters. The entire propaganda is aimed at impressing the voters. The empty promises, the inducements in cash or kind, the accusations and the emotional speeches in public meetings etc., are the means they adopt in this process. The non-conventional approach in this regard is a collaborative effort with journalists to impress the target groups through the media. Hence an "impressionist" approach to agenda setting may well suit the above discussed conditions and serve the purposes of political parties too. This approach can be defined as a method of media propaganda aimed at moulding voting pattern in a desirable direction by impressing or influencing the emotions of the electorate. "Impressionist" approach covers the characteristics of the above discussed conditions to some extent and also helps to cope up with the conditions of the emotional model. The scope of this approach is very wide and enables the politicians and media personnel to design their strategies according to the changing patterns of voters' interests. The target group for this approach is usually as observed by the researchers the "uninformed, uneducated and gullible voter".

Impressionism has both positive and negative features. The distinction between emotions and attitudes is of some importance here. Compared to attitudes, emotions are relatively more temporary. During elections where the outcome is more important than the means, the temptation to use the impressionist approach to appeal to the emotions is more than influencing attitudes. This would not however make the approach narrow nor the media limited to superficial programming. In its broad sense "Impressionist approach" in election broadcasts can lead to more discernible political education of the rural folk and help them in making voting decisions. The response could be large and massive when it plays on the right emotions and sentiments leading to unexpected swings and waves. However, it may depend heavily on the creativity and the wit of journalists and producers of the media. An impressionist agenda would certainly address a large segment of voters who are certainly not covered and catered to by the other four approaches.

How far these theories are applicable in the Indian context? The representatives' positive response to the potential of Broadcast media and the noticeable changes in the present political programmes on Television may definitely open the doors for more research in this field. However, extensive programming at regional levels should be given consideration in view of the linguistic diversities in India. Apart from this, political scientists observe great changes in the voters' behaviour over the years. The declining proportion of votes, the increasing volatility, the weakening of party loyalties, increased attention to issues, media effects etc., are the major contributing factors to these changes. Factors like multiple party system and brevity of electoral cycles (due to frequent dissolvement of legislatures and parliament), increasing defections among parties, failure of alternate governments in solving the problems etc., are making voters apathetic to elections. Explaining the negative influence of frequent elections on the minds of the voters, Laver[5] says "in most western countries the life of a government is a few years at the most, and its effective life is shorter still, for in its later months the thoughts of ministers turn towards the coming election". He quotes Aristotle who argued in his "Politics" for a short period in office, in order to limit the damage that a politician could do. But Laver opines that it also limits the good and the opportunities· afforded to ordinary citizens to participate in government are infrequent and cursory enough not to argue for a longer gap between elections. Our sense of political impotence is strengthened when the information technology systems of government departments and large corporations hold the data needed to support analysis. In consequence, most ordinary men and women simply drop out into a condition of fatalistic apathy, leaving political life to the minority who find it rewarding, while they turn to private pastimes where they can make their mark, achieve recognition and be valued for their visible individual contributions".

From a broadcaster's point of view, these research findings would be of some help to the policy makers and producers in making party broadcasts and in maintaining accuracy and objectivity in the programmes. Especially the 'bias' in political broadcasts can be minimized to a great extent if the contributing factors are identified and dealt carefully.

REFERENCES

1. Harrop, Martin—Voting and the electorate Drucker, Henry *et al., Developments in British Politics* : London Mac Millan, 1983, pp. 36, 41 & 46.
2. *Ibid* pp. 44 & 45.
3. Blumler, Jay G., Gurevitch, Michael and Nossiter T.J.—Setting the television news agenda, campaign observation at the BBC. Crewe, Ivor and Harrops, Martin : *Political Communications—The general election campaign of 1983*, Cambridge, Cambridge University Press, 1986, pp. 114, 115 & 119.

4. Blumler, Jay G., *The political effects of mass communications*, The audience unit 8, The Open University Social Sciences a third level course, Milton Keyness Walton Hall, pp. 37 & 38.
5. Laver Murray : *Information Technology—Agent of Change*; Cambridge, Cambridge University Press, 1989.

Chapter 11

SUMMARY/CONCLUSIONS

Politics is a vast subject and party system in democracy is one specialized area. Voters need to be well informed to be able to analyse day-to-day political developments. Even to the intelligentia it is rather difficult to judge the nuances of the politics. The plight of the rural masses in this respect can well be imagined. Time is another factor. Political parties have the responsibility of enlightening the voters by simplifying these changes and enabling them to choose right persons to represent them. In this process, mass media play a pivotal role as non-formal educational institution. Whether it is regular news bulletins, current affairs or party broadcasts, the purpose remains unchanged. Party broadcasts occupy a unique position in political broadcasting since they are expected to have a bearing on voters' decisions. The preceding analysis was an attempt to study in depth the role of Radio and Television as election media with the help of a detailed questionnaire.

What are the present conditions? Can we improve them? What ought to be the ideal situation? What could be expected in future? The discussion mainly covered these perspectives in addition to the politicians' conceptions about the media and their target audience-based on the responses. The analysis of politicians' perceptions about the role of broadcast media in party politics can be claimed as one of the important aspects of the study. Some additional information related to these aspects was elicited from the respondents and the arguments presented. A partywise analysis of the views of the respondents, discussion of significant minority responses and individual opinions of the politicians have been carried out in the discussion and the influence of major socio-economic factors like Age and Position were given due consideration.

The following are the broad conclusions of the study

(1) A comparative look into the data on the impact of election broadcasts on voters revealed progressive change from negative response to positive from the past to the future.

(2) "Commitment followed by "along the wave" were claimed as the determinants of the voting pattern. Propaganda effect secured third place.

(3) The leaders were quite content with the present system of broadcasts except in two aspects i.e. the quantum and duration of the programmes. Editing the script by media officials was resented by a significant group.

One would observe a general dissatisfaction among political parties over policies of political coverage on Radio/TV. The respondents unanimity in their desire for maintaining orderliness and discipline in matters relating to political publicity was very clear from the study, though surprising.

(4) Door-to-door campaign followed by press and Television were rated as the most influential media during elections by majority of the leaders. They did not categorically mention any medium to be superior to other but critically weighed the strengths and weak points of each system. The main basis for their judgement seemed to be the role played by each medium in the present political context.

(5) The political leaders were clear that rural masses were moderately knowledgeable to appreciate

the media campaigning but were more positive to political messages through Radio/TV than the urban. Intellectuals among men and housewives among women paid more attention to PBs. Influence of age on the responses was quite significant. Elders differed with others showing high level consistency in their conceptions about audience.

(6) As discussed earlier the leaders could not relate the behaviour of audience to PBs satisfactorily. This is quite understandable as their participation in PBs till now was very less and they might have not felt the need to concentrate on audience behaviour etc. When the politicians regularly participate in media programmes especially on Radio/TV and give more importance to feedback and evaluation, not only their understanding of media habits may increase but could also present good election programmes.

(7) The partymen desired changes in the present set-up except in the denial of opportunity to unrecognised political parties and independents. They made reasonable suggestions for better presentation of election appeals over Radio/TV. Voters court followed by debate between the candidates were selected as the suitable formats for PBs. More prominence to party symbol, visuals in presentations, analysis of party manifestos were also proposed. Political advertising did not receive much support.

(8) For many politicians, Radio and TV promoted only passive learning among the electorates. They also differed on the issue of political parties accusing each other over media and its impact on the voters. Majority believed in Broadcast media's capability in leading masses into active political participation. They also gave credit to this medium for breaking barriers in reaching the remote voters. Regarding Radio/TV maintaining non-partisan stance in party conflict, a

ruling and opposition division was prominently observed among the respondents. The power of TV as a political medium in giving publicity to less established contenders was recognised by a majority of the politicians. However, they partially accepted the observation that the unsophistication of voters and politicians may pose difficulties in programme making over Radio/TV. Regarding empty promises of politicians causing damage to the credibility of the media the majority assessed the harm to be significant while the number who thought the opposite was also quite sizeable. Many agreed that failure in implementing the election promises committed over media led to frustration amongst the rural masses.

(9) Partywise Analysis

The analysis revealed some partywise similarities as also differences in the opinions of the leaders. Parties agreed on certain issues had divergent ideas on other aspects. Minority opinions in the respective parties were unexpected but thought provoking in many cases.

The BJP and Communists in general tended to prefer ideal situations. This perhaps may be because they never had the opportunity to rule the state or anywhere in sight of such a possibility and therefore may not be aware of the hard realities in running the official machinery. As active opposition parties they were always engaged in criticizing the pitfalls and shortcomings of the ruling parties. On certain matters related to the media, BJP reposed more faith in the power and potentiality of Radio and TV. BJP seemed to be more favourable to new and innovative thoughts at least on experimental basis whereas Communists were content what the existing practice. The Congress (I)'s lukewarm interest in new ideas may be due to their long standing association with the government and their caution against taking risk with experimental approaches.

The variations in the sample's opinion creates an impression that the parties as cohesive groups are not having any strong conviction or concrete opinion on many issues related to media. Only BJP whose responses were unanimous on many issues and sometimes Communists, reveal firm attitudes and ideas about media.

(10) Influence of Age

The agewise analysis revealed a steady deviation of opinion between the three age groups especially amongst elders. Generally, opinions and ideas of persons about different issues or aspects firm up as the age moves on as seen in the case of senior politicians in this study. This could be one reason for the elders differing with others. Since the difference is visible in almost all the questions this can be attributed to the age. The consistency in the responses without many contradictions among the groups belonging to different age intervals is also remarkable.

Eventhough no strong reasons could be given for the observed influence of age the following remarks may summarise the attitudes of the three age groups and their varied responses in assessing the utility and effects of PBs.

Elders

Elders seem to be more thoughtful and critical in their approach although their outlook on Broadcast media and politics was generally conventional. A high level of consistency and integrity in responses was noticed from question to question including those aimed at cross checking. The elders were particularly more concerned about the unwanted effects of media in the political spectrum. The feed-back also reflected their low concern in areas like introducing innovative techniques and methods in the present setup. Any innovation may not be of much use to them since they have already reached the final stage of their political career. Few elders were reluctant to answer the questionnaire in spite of repeated persuasion. A trace of "not to compromise" with the present mode of political life compared to the standards of olden periods was also prominently noticed among these persons. However, the researcher is happy that a good amount of credit goes to the elders from whose active responses, constructive criticism, practical approach and suggestions, some valid observations could be made.

Middle Age Group

This section of the sample mostly consisted of ministers, ex-ministers, MPs and active politicians. They seem to have assessed the value of PBs in terms of their use in the present context especially in supplementing their campaigning efforts during polls. As discussed earlier their estimation of the potential of Radio and TV as campaign tools is very high, but they seem to be disappointed for not being able to use them extensively to suit their political requirements. This group was more positive and cooperative during interviews and expressed eagerness to substitue other modes of election campaigning with Broadcast media. They are the best channels to interact with the voters, as recognized and practiced in some foreign countries— the sample thought. The middle aged politicians discussed the issues with a pragmatic approach.

Youngsters

Youngsters were more enthusiastic, quite open to new ideas and changes in the present set-up. Many youngsters actively discussed the subject from different angles with the researcher. They have also expressed more optimism for Radio/TV as rescues from tedious campaigning schedules.

(11) Influence of Position

This could be traced only on a very few aspects of the study compared to age the influence of which is spread over almost all the aspects/areas even though the effect was less. The reason may be explained as below. Age is a biological factor and position a sociological. Maturity, related with age, is an attribute of the individual (respondent) that can have influence on any aspect, whereas the position being a social factor can make the influence on its related field only. The area being politics in the present study only. The such questions that have bearing on the political status of a leader have exhibited the influence of position unlike the other variable, age whose influence was all pervasive. However like age, the effect of position was more noticeable in some areas and less in certain others.

In the fourth and fifth parts of the questionnaire the influence of position was noticed only in a few areas. Ministers were more positive in their responses in certain areas. This can be related to the general notion that success brings happiness and makes one see things in a positive perspective.

The difference in the responses positionwise has also revealed the nature of ruling and opposition. As mentioned earlier, ministers represented ruling party's views and non-ministers, the opposition's. Another factor supporting this observation in that AP Congress has been ruling the state for a marathon period (38 years) except for a few years when TDP was in power. Most of the ministers interviewed belonged to Congress (I) and only a small number to TDP. This indicates that majority of the non-ministers largely are from TDP and some to BJP and Communist parties and a few from Cong (I).

On the whole the variations in the responses according to the age and position of the sample stress once again the need to consider the role of socio-economic variables in impact assessment studies without which generalizations may not be very valid.

(12) It was surprising that some of the politicians feigned ignorance of the fact that Radio/TV are extending campaigning facility during the elections and were happy to know it through the researcher. This was observed during the preliminary contacts before administering the questionnaire.

The discussion can be summed up with two more individual observations in this regard. They are (1) The socio-demographic differences among urban and rural population may also influence the impact of party broadcasts. The effect of these programmes is not similar in urban and rural areas. Rural masses prefer personal contact. It may take some time for them to get accustomed to media campaigning—the sample opined. (2) Leaders are sceptical about the applicability of this kind of research in the actual ground.

The study has identified politicians as important persons in the process of political communications especially during elections and studied their perceptions on various aspects of party campaining through radio/TV. The above conclusions broadly reflect their opinions about the present system, and hopes for the future. The study recommends the policy makers to consider these views while designing the programmes.

As is well known during the 1991 midterm elections to Lok Sabha, violence dominated the election scenario. The amount of money spent by the individuals as well as by the respective parties was also very large. In addition to all the observations one point that was unanimously agreed by the sample was that it is really good if the entire election campaigning is done only through electronic media i.e. Radio and TV. The sample themselves pointed out that the politicians have to undertake extensive touring during campaigning. Even though the campaign commences well in advance, they were not able to cover the entire constituency, whereas through electronic media they could reach even the remote corners of their area. The second reason put forward was that people with money power are able to induce the voters in many ways, but in Radio/Television campaigning this practice can be totally curbed, a dangerous evil during every election can be avoided or atleast minimised through media campaigning.

The sample, specifically citing late Rajiv Gandhi's assasination, expressed deep concern for the amount of violence that has increased over the years and spread everywhere in the country. They are also very hopeful that media campaigning is the only solution to such unhealthy and destructive activities.

In addition to this, official manpower and machinery used in campaigning especially to arrange public meetings etc (often official machinery is misused by ruling party as alleged by the opposition parties) can be avoided and better utilised elsewhere.

Media campaigning minimizes group activity and promotes individual effort. In the present society where politics and violence have become inseparable people have high hopes on media campaigning for solving such issues. However, this is possible only when media give enough coverage and people appreciate media campaigning to other forms. Some leaders perceived that rural voters prefer personal contact and may not like mechanical and distant communication, but some argued when people are habituated to listen to/watch the President, Prime Minister and Chief Minister's broadcasts, in days to come, they may also get used to election campaigning through media. While media are not free from criticism the argument can be concluded with Gamble and Gamble's[1] observation in the developed countries. They feel news organizations serve as "mediators" between the government and the governed : whenever the government wants the people to know or do something, it relies on the media to relay the message. In the same way, whenever citizens want to find out something about their government they almost always rely on the media to provide the answer. This role can give the mass communication organisations great power, because in deciding what messages to relay and how information is to be presented, these organisations determine what issues will be discussed in national politics.

On the whole the politicians strongly advocated change in the party system and election campaigning during discussions. They favoured two party system all over the country and no other means except extensive media campaigning.

Political Programmes on Media

As critics observe, media give more importance to programming during elections and political turmoils. But these programmes may have little effect on the people. A planned and cumulative programming on political education over media throughout the year will definitely have long term impact on the audience and may supplement their knowledge during elections.

This also promotes better understanding of media programmes. The present news and current affairs programmes serve only information purposes. Voting is an act that involves decision making which includes conflictual thinking. This again requires higher knowledge about the issues. In addition many socio-economic factors play a role in the process of voting. Hence there is a need to develop well planned methodical information systems to make the voter act rationally. Party broadcasts are occasional programmes which come once in long years depending upon the political system adopted in a particular country. While assessing the impact of these broadcasts the role of regular political programmes over media throughout the years i.e. news and current affairs are also of much significance.

However from a research angle election period is claimed as the most appropriate time for studies. There are some advantages and disadvantages in relying heavily upon the evidence drawn from election campaign alone. As observed by Blumler[2] Itheiel-de Sola Pool opines that :

> "elections among other things are a laboratory. He meant by this that we usually know when an election will be held enabling researchers to prepare their field work thoroughly in advance. The form, the outcome will take, the casting of votes for alternative candidates or parties—is not only known well, but is typically exact, measurable and readily related to measures of other variables. Since that form does not change with the passage of time, findings of a succession of campaign studies can be conveniently compared with each other. And finally, since the election campaign is an occasion for the launching of intensive attempts

at persuasion the researchers can observe not only how voters react to the various political offerings but they can also put their theories about such processes to a stringent empirical test. But many analysts do not suppose that voting as such is the only political act worthy of study form a communication stand point. The limitations of this focus are it directs attention to short term effects (over the campaign period) at the expense of the more gradual cumulation over a large span of time of media influences on people's political beliefs. Another is that it deals only with manifestly political messages and ignores the more diffuse but possibly more pervasive ideological implications of other forms of media content such as soap operas, family comedies, adventure serials, advertisements etc."

However, attempts were made by the researchers in the past to counteract these limitations.

Communication research is slowly but steadily gaining momentum in India also. Particularly with the advent of television the impact assessment studies are increasing. Research especially in the form of immediate feed-back and evaluation is slowly becoming a part of all the systems for better planning. And computer technology is making this task more easier. The sample's hopes about Radio and TV in future politics indicates the role they can enact in the days to come. Especially as Boyd[3] observes "TV is credited with almost superhuman powers. It can, they say, start wars, and it can sap the will to continue these wars. It can polarise society, and it can prevent society talking sensibly to itself. It can cause trouble on the streets".

REFERENCES

1. Gamble, Michael W., and Gamble, Teri Kwal; *Introducing Mass Communication*, Singapore, McGraw Hill Book Co., 1989 pp. 400 & 401.
2. Blumler, Jay G.; *The Political Effects of Mass Communication*, The audience Unit 8; The Open University Social Sciences a third level course, Milton Keyness Walton Hall p. 13.
3. Boyd, Andrew; *Broadcast Journalism—Techniques of Radio and T.V. News*. Oxford, Heinmann Professional Publishing Ltd.

QUESTIONNAIRE

From :

Dr. P.V. Sharada
B.Sc., M.A. (Phi), M.Ed., Ph.D (OSM)

Sir/Madam,

This questionnaire seeks to find out your opinion about the present Party Broadcasts over Radio/ Television and your perceptions about the role of Broadcast media in Party Politics. I request your cooperation in answering the questions before the election results are announced and assure you that the information given will be kept in confidence and used for research purpose only.

Name :

Age :

Position :

M.L.A.

M.P.

Minister/Ex-Minister

Party Worker with position

Party worker without position :

Others :

Duration served :

PART-I

Present Party Broadcasts—Merits and Demerits

(1) Which media unit in your opinion influences the voters most? Give your preference as 1, 2, 3 against each.

Press	Radio
Films	Television
Audio & Video Cassettes	Wall posters/Pamphlets/leaflets
Door-to-door Campaign	Public meetings

(2) To what extent do you think that pre-election broadcasts influenced the voters in the past?

To some extent	Very little
To a great extent	Not at all

(3) Are you satisfied with the quantum of party broadcasts i.e., once over television and twice over All India Radio?

Yes	No

If no, what would be the ideal frequency, after the elections are notified?

Once	Twice
Once a week	Once a fortnight

What would be the ideal duration in your opinion for party Broadcasts?

5-10 minutes	10-15 minutes
15-20 minutes	20-30 minutes

more than 30 minutes

(4) Are you happy with the present timings of party broadcasts over Radio/Television?

Yes	No

If no, would you suggest any modification in the timings?

Suggestion

(5) Do you feel that the present system of giving equal opportunity and time on Radio/Television to both bigger and smaller parties is reasonable?

Yes No

If no, what is your suggestion?

Please write here :

(6) Is enough freedom is being given to express party's views in the present frame-work of party broadcasts?

Yes No

(7) What is your opinion about the election code for party broadcasts?

Desirable Not Desirable

If desirable, who should form the code for party broadcasts?

Government Media officials

All Party Committee Public Committee

(8) Do you think editing the script is necessary in party broadcasts?

(a) Necessary (b) Not necessary

If not necessary, should these aspects be allowed in party broadcasts?

	Yes	No
(a) Economic Offences		
(b) Political Offences		
(c) Criminal conduct		
(d) Slanderous personal allegations		

(9) Why do you agree to give party broadcast over Radio/TV? Please rank them according to your preference as 1, 2, 3 etc.

(a) Broadcast media is more effective compared to other media of mass communications .....
(b) Because the facility is available..........
(c) To reach more people in less time..........
(d) Glamour of the media attracts me..........
(e) Because other parties are availing the facility..........
(f) No financial implications..........
(g) Others (Please specify)

(10) Whose guidance/suggestions you take into consideration before giving a party broadcast? Please rank them as 1, 2, 3.

Media researchers	Listeners/viewers
Intellectuals	Party Leaders/Party Workers

(11) How do you choose a person for party broadcast? Please rank your order of preference as 1, 2, 3 etc.

Oratory	Standing in the party
Popularity among the public	Intellectual appeal

(12) In your opinion what are the factors that influence the voters? Please rank your preference as 1, 2, 3 etc.

(a) *Party*

Party policies programmes and manifesto :
Party performance in the past :
Caliber of leaders in a party :
Party organisation and cadre :
Party symbol :

(b) *Candidate*

Education	Caste
Religion	Honesty/Integrity
Performance in the past	

(c) *Publicity*

Media propaganda	Public meetings
Media advertisement	Any other (Pl. specify)

(13) It is observed that the film personalities are able to win more votes in the recent past elections. What could be the reason?
Please give reasons in order of preference as 1, 2, 3 etc.
- (a) Extensive media exposure
- (b) Political image created by the medium
- (c) Their genuine activities and concern for the masses
- (d) Hero-worship promoted by the medium
- (e) Glamorous image
- (f) Their political awareness/maturity

(14) At present audio and video cassettes are heavily used during the elections. What could be the reason for this?
Please rank your preference as 1, 2, 3 etc.
- (a) They are more effective means to reach the voters
- (b) Broadcast media is not giving enough publicity/time/scope
- (c) They can be repeated as many times as required
- (d) Freedom of expression of political view

(15) There is a strong feeling among the voters that politicians generally make empty promises in media campaigning. How do you rate?

Usually	Occasionally
Rarely	Never

PART-II

Conceptions about the Audience

(16) Do you think that pre-election broadcast will have any impact on the audience/viewers?

To some extent	To a great extent
Very little	Not at all

(17) Do you think our Rural Folk are knowledgeable enough to appreciate the broadcast media campaigning?

Highly knowledgeable	Moderately knowledgeable
Not knowledgeable	Cannot say

(18) Which of the following audience are likely to get more influenced by party broadcasts than others?

Please rank your preference as 1, 2, 3 etc.

Heavy viewers/listeners

Medium viewers/listeners

Light viewers/listeners

(19) Which type of audience in your opinion shows more interest in the broadcasts?

Committed voters	Non-committed voters
Voters with general interest in politics	Don't know

(20) Among men which of the following professions are more affected by the party broadcasts?

Intellectuals	Businessmen
Employees	Labour

(20a) To which of the following categories of women party broadcasts appeal most?

House-wife	Working women
Youth	Labour

(21) Whose response in your opinion is more positive to political messages through broadcast media?
(a) Rural masses
(b) Urban masses
(c) Don't know

(22) In your opinion which in order of rating determine the voting pattern of a voter?

Intelligence	Intuition
Commitment	Propaganda effect
Along the wave	Inducements in cash or kind

PART-III

Improvements within the Present Setup

(23) Do you think that the unrecognised political parties and independents also should be given opportunity over Radio/TV?

Yes	No

(24) Which type of the media programme in your opinion is the most suitable type for party political broadcasts?
(a) Talk
(b) Interview
(c) Panel discussion
(d) Voter's court (Candidates area questioned by selected voters)
(e) Debate between the candidates

(25) Do you think that the symbol of the party should be given prominence in the party broadcasts?

Necessary	Necessary to some extent
Not necessary	Don't know

(26) Do you feel advertisement by parties through Radio/TV will give more effective results?

Very much	Somewhat
Not much	Don't know

(27) Do you think party broadcasts over television should be supported by visuals and films?

Yes   No

PART-IV

Some Perceptions about the "Broadcast Media and Politics"

(28) In the process of political communication broadcast media with its greater reach to the less educated part of the electorate promotes :

Passive learning (Slow learning)
Active learning
Creative learning
No learning at all

(29) Party broadcasts over Radio/Television are reaching a sector of voters who were previously more difficult to reach. Do you agree?

Agree   Strongly agree
Disagree   Strongly disagree
Don't know

(30) Broadcast media being a domestic media can bring political messages into the home environment. This may lead to further discussion in the home which may in turn lead to active political participation later. Is this happening now?

Great deal   Not much
Somewhat   Don't know

(31) Broadcast media maintains non-partisan stance in its relationship to party political conflict and maintains fairness, impartiality and neutrality. What extent do you agree with this image of the media?

To some extent   Not at all
To a great extent   Don't know

(32) Communication researchers opine that television as a political medium occasionally gives publicity

boost to certain less established contenders. Do you agree?

Agree | Disagree
Strongly agree | Strongly disagree
Don't know

(33) It is often said that certain amount of political unsophistication is present both among the voters and politicians in our country. This may make broadcast media campaigning difficult exercise. What do you say?

Very difficult | Somewhat difficult
It depends | Not difficult at all

(34) It is often said that politicians in media campaigns concentrate more on accusing each other. What response will it generate among the audience?

(a) It generates interest (b) It generates controversy
(c) It generates disinterest (d) It is not ethical

(35) Broadcast media claims more credibility when compared with other media of mass communications. Do you think this credibility could be damaged in long run if it allows politicians to go on with their empty promises?

To some extent | To a great extent
Not at all | Don't know

(36) Communication researchers have observed that media campaigning raises aspirations and when politicians fail to fulfil the promises, it leads to frustration especially amongst the rural voters. Do you agree?

Agree | Disagree
Strongly disagree | Strongly agree
Don't know

PART-V

Future Expectations

(37) Which medium in your opinion will be more helpful to persons who aspire for a political career in future?

Films Television
Radio Newspapers
Others

(38) Do you expect local Radios to play an active role in future politics?

Yes No

If yes, to what extent?

Major Minor
Nil Don't know

(39) Do you think that the party broadcasts in future should be followed by an analysis or discussion by eminent political thinkers?

Yes No

If yes, what type of analysis would you prefer? Please rank them according to your preference.

(a) Analysis of party broadcasts
(b) Analysis of party manifesto
(c) Analysis of political leadership
(d) Any other opinion (Please specify)

(40) Do you think that the Radio and Television will in future be able to influence the most deep-seated political attitudes of the voters?

To some extent To a great extent
Very little Not at all

(41) Do you plan to listen/watch the broadcasts of political parties other than your own?

Yes No

BIBLIOGRAPHY

Baruah, U.L., *This is All India Radio.* New Delhi, Publications Division, Ministry of Information and Broadcasting, Government of India, 1983).

Barwise, Patric and Ehrenbergh, Andrew : *Television and its Audience.* London : SAGE, 1988.

Blumler, Jay. G., *The Political Effects of Mass-communication : Audience Unit 8,* The Open University Social Sciences a third level course, Milton Keyness Walton Hall.

Bower, T. Robert, *Television and the Public.* New York : Columbia University Press, 1985.

Boyd, Andrew : *Broadcast Journalism—Techniques of Radio and TV News.* Oxford : Heinmann Professional Publishing Ltd.

Casty Alan, *Mass-media and Mass-man.* Holt, Rinehart and Winston. East Sussex, 1973.

Chalapathi Rao, *Journalism and Politics,* New Delhi : Vikas Publishing House, 1984.

Clutter Buck, *The Media and Political Violence,* London : MacMillan, 1983.

Cockrell, Michael, Live from No. 10 : *The Inside Story of Prime Ministers and Television,* London : Faber and Faber Ltd., 1983.

Crewe, Ivor and Harrop, Martin, (Ed). *Political Communication : The General Election Campaign of 1983,* Cambridge : Cambridge University Press, 1986.

Crick, Bernard and Porter Alex, *Political Education and Political Literacy.* London : Longman Group Limited, 1978.

Diamond Edwin. *Television, Politics and the News* Cambridge : MIT Press, 1977.

Drucker, Henry *et al.*, *Developments in British Politics*. London : Macmillan Education Ltd, 1983.

Gamble, Michael W. and Gamble, Teri Kwal. *Introducing Mass Communication.* Singapore : McGraw Hill Book Co., 1989.

Gurevitch Michael and Blumler Jay G., *Linkage Between the Mass Media and Politics—A Model for the Analysis of Political Communication System.* Leeds : University of Leeds Press, 1978.

Laver, Murray, *Information Technology—Agent of Change,* Cambridge : Cambridge University Press, 1989.

Long, E. Gladys, Long, Kurt, *Politics and Television Reviewed.* Chicago : Quadrangle Books, 1968.

Long, Kurt and Long, Engel, Gladys. *Voting and Non-voting Implications of Broadcasting Returns before Polls are Closed.* New York : Columbia University Press, 1983.

Mueller Claus, *The Politics and Communication—A Study in the Political Sociology of Language, Socialization and Legitimation.* New York : Oxford University Press, 1974.

Mukharjee, B.N., *Mass Media and Political Modernity : An Empirical Study of Five Developing Countries.* Agra : National Psychological Corporation, 1979.

Pye, W. Lucian (Ed.), *Communications and Political Development,* (Studies in Political Development, Vol. I) Princeton, New Jersey : Princeton University Press : Lawrenceville, 1963.

Robinson, J. Michael, *Television and American Politics 1956-76.* New Delhi : United States Information Services.

Rose, Richard and Mc Allister, Ian. V*oters begin to Choose from Closed Class to Open Elections in Britain.* London : Sage Publications, 1986.

Schramme, Wilbur, *Mass-media and National Development.* California : Stanford University Press, 1964.

Smith, Anthony (Ed.), *Television and Political Life—Studies in Six European Countries*. London : MacMillan, 1979.

Snow, S. Marcellus, *International Commercial Satellite Communications—Economic and Political Issues of the first decade of INTELSAT*. New York : Praeger Publishers.

Sharada, P.V., *Impact of Television on the Political Awareness of Rural Masses*. New Delhi : Gyan Publishing House, 1992.

Swallo, Norman, *Factual Television—Television and Party Politics*, London : Focal Press, 1966.

Thomas, Ruth, *Broadcasting and Democracy in France*. New York : Beekman Publishers, 1976.

Tracey, Michael, *The Production of Political Television*. London : Routledge and Kegan Paul.

Tyrrel, Robert, *The Work of the Television Journalist*. London : Focal Press, 1972.

Ure, C.S., *The Political Impact of Mass Media*. London : Constable and Co.

Walter, Debbie, *The Polls and Polling Day : Why didn't U.K. voters do what the Research Samples Say they would?* "ADMAP" July/August 1992.

INDEX

Accusation, 112, 113, 117, 149, 153
Active learning, 98
Active politics, 102
Advantages, 41, 48
Advertisements, 1, 9, 77
Agenda, 34
Agenda setting, 145,
  mechanism, 34
  theory, 81
Agreement, 98, 99, 100, 103, 107
AIR autonomy, 4
Allegations, 28, 30, 32
American Presidential elections, 91
Andhra Pradesh, 39, 52
Andhra Pradesh State Assembly, 13
Aristotle, 155
Aspirations, 115-116
Atkinson, Max, 90
Audience,
  categorisation of, 57
  types of, 51-53
Audience Research Unit of Delhi Doordarshan 7,
Audio-vidio Cassettes, 41-42

Baruah, U.L., 11
Barwise, Patrick, 48, 102
Becker, 82, 126
BJP, 13, 19, 30, 39, 43, 45, 46, 98, 101, 102
Blumler, J.G., 1, 2, 56, 81, 99, 127, 158, 170
Bofors, issue of, 30
Boost publicity, 108, 109
Boyd, Andrews, 70, 109, 172
British Broadcast Media, 71
British elections, 127
British television's political coverage, 80
Broadcast media, 3, 15, 36
  and politics, perceptions, 173-74
  autonomy of, 17
  campaigning, 14, 110
  credibility of, 114-115
  facilities, 11-12
  learning promoted, 98
  non-partisan stance, 106-107
  objectives, 45-46
  potentiality of, 36
  timings of, 24
Byrness, 82

Campaign programmes, 70
Candidate's performance, 131, 138
Cartwright, 17
Cinema gimmicks, 39
Clinton, challenges, 89
Cockerell, Michael, 71, 108, 116
Commitments, 141, 142, 143, 159, 160
Committed voters, 53-55
Communal riots, 79
Communication,
  channels, 7
  research, 172
  technology, 33
Communist parties, 19, 39
Conceptions, 51, 171
Congress (I) 13, 23, 24, 26, 28, 29, 30, 39, 43, 105
Constraints, 16, 92
Consumerism, 84

Consumption factors, 48
Crises, 80
Criminal offences, 32
Creative learning, 98, 99
Credibility, 114, 118
Criticisms, 2, 26, 36, 47, 80, 104, 106, 108, 114, 117, 145, 164
Current affairs programmes, 170

Data,
  party-wise analysis, 17-18
Democracy, 37, 117, 157
Deviation, 17
Domestic media, 101, 102
Doordarshan, autonomy of, 4
Door-to-door campaign, 45, 50, 132, 159
Dunleavy, Patrick, 130, 131

Educational programmes, 83
Edward, Heath, 71, 117, 128
Ehrenberg, Andrew, 98, 102
Elections, 1
  media coverage of, 149-50
Election agenda setting, approaches, 158-59
Election Broadcast, 11-20
  empty promises of, 93-94
  objectives, 12-13
    minority responses, 18-19
    samples 13
    tools, 18
Election campaigns, 2-8, 36
  in urban and rural areas, 7-8
  mechanism of, 34
  types of, 1-12
Election code, 28-29
Election Commission, 11, 26
Election news, coverage of, 104
Election promises, 91-92
  propaganda, 6
  symbols, 11
Electronic media, 5, 167
Emotional speeches, 153
Emotionalism, 143
Erbring, 151

Family socialization, 140, 141
Film stars, 37, 38
Frostration, 116, 118
Freedom of expression, 26-28
Funds, 9
Future expectations, 175-76

Gamble, Michael W., 3, 66, 87, 96, 168
Goldenberg, 151
Good poll ratings, 87

Harijans, 6
Harrop, Martin, 127, 128, 144
  valing models, 140
Heavy viewers, 53
Himmelweit, 128
Hero-worship, 41
Hypothesis, 6

Ideological interpretations, 128
Illiterate female, 6
Illiteracy, 144
Impressionist approach, 155
Indian voting behaviour, 153
Individual observations, 166
Individual opinions, 17, 18, 64-65, 77
Inducement, 136
Influence of Age, 163-64
Influence of position, 165-66
Intellectuals, 63, 65
Interpersonal communication, 8
  channels, 51
Issue voting model, 140, 142, 151

Janta Party Government, 11

Laver, Murray, 88, 89, 155
Local radios in politics, 43-44
Lok Sabha election, 1971, 5
  1980, 7
  1971, 13

Magic-bullet theory, 96
Manifestos, 94, 128, 138
Mass communication, 96
Mass Communication Organisations, 168
Mass education, 45
Mass media,
  effects of, 3
Maya, 80
McAllister, Ian, 33, 54
McCombs, 126
Mcteod, 82
McLeod, 126
Media,
  advertisement, 133
  effects model, 126
  political prgrammes of, 168-69
  propaganda, 132
Mediamen, 97
Medium viewers, 53
Mencker, H.L., 17
Michael Foot, 89
Mid-term poll, 1991, 13, 167
Miller, 151
Minority responses, 18-19
Mobile political sentiments, 114
Most influential media Unit, 34
Multi-media campaign, 33-50
Multi-media competition, 34

Narula, Uma, 7
National integration, 6
Neutral voters, 14
Newspapers, 6, 50
News programme, 47
Non-committed voters, 33, 55
Non-partisan stance, 103

Objectives, 12-13
Observations, 67, 89, 115, 118-19
Occasional programmes, 170
One-way communication system, 41
Opinion, 21, 22, 54, 55
  polls, 87, 88
Oratory, 90

Pack Journalism, 49 .
Panel discussion, 75
Party Broadcasts,
  analysis of, 81-82
  commencement of, 26
  duration of, 23-24
  effect of, 124-25
  election code, 28
  freedom of expression, 26-27
  formats for, 69-70
  frequency of, 21-22
  guidance for, 85-86
  influence of, 122
  preferences for, 38
  politician listen, 137
  political leadership in, 84-85
  quantum of, 22
  scrip editing, 29-30
  timings of, 24-25
  types of analysis, 83-84
  women's response to, 63-64
Party-telecasts, visuals in, 78-79
Party, identification models, 140, 142
  ideology, 17
  manifestos, 94, 128

performance, 124
policies and programme, 129
propaganda, 6, 15
symbal, 74-75, 132
Party-wise analysis, 58, 162-63
differences, 32
Passive learning, 98
Perceptions, 16, 96, 127
Personal discussion, 32
Pervasiveness poses problems, 100
Political,
accusation, 113
advertisement, 15-16, 160
effect of, 77
attitudes, 121-24
communications, 58,66
role of, 3
research, 1
theory, 96
education, 7
jingles, 76
medium, 107-108
messages, 59, 63-65
programme, 16
socialisation, 6
unsophistication, 110-12
Politicians, types of, 19
Pre-election broadcasts, 123-25
Present party broadcast, 167
President Bush, 88
Press, 9, 35, 36
Press and Television, preference for, 47-48
Private polls, 89
Production factors, 48
Promoting future political career, 46
Propaganda, 12, 67
effect, 134, 136-37, 157
mode of, 47
Public Committee, 29
Public meetings, 5, 6, 9, 36, 111
Public opinion polls, 134
Publicity, 132-33
mode of, 42

Questions, 15, 16, 18
Questionnaire, 15, 24, 121, 166

Radclife, 70
Radical model, 140,142
Radio and TV,
broadcast facilities, 12
limitation of, 41
pervasive nature of, 100
political effects of, 96-97
promises and credibility of, 114-115
Rajiv Gandhi's assassination, 14, 167
Rasis aspirations, 115
Recognized parties, 21
Restrictions, 28
Robinson, 149
Rose, Richard, 33, 54
Rural masses, 51,62, 166
Rural-urban difference, 58-59
Rural voters, 9, 45, 116

Satellite Instructional Television Experiment (SITE), 6
Schramme, Wilbur, 116
Script editing, 29-30, 32
Second World War, 1
Self-criticism, 93
Sharada, P.V., 166
Socio-economic factors, 157
State Assembly elections, 1977, 11

Talkback systems, 49
Television on Rural masses, 9
TV's dominations, 47-48
Telugu Desam Party (TDP), 13, 15, 34, 39, 43, 45, 46, 52, 98
Two-way communication system, 41
Tyrrel, Robert, 48

Unknown voters, 100, 101
Unrecognised political parties, 67-68
Unsophistication, 161
  problem of, 110, 117
Urban areas, 7
  masses, 51
Ure, C.S, 1, 14

Variables, 17, 18
Visual programmes, 67
Vote grabbers, 37-38
Voters Court, 73, 160
Voters, 8, 9, 36
  dissatisfaction, 130
  factors influencing of, 127-28, 131-33
  political attitudes of, 125-26
Voting behaviour, 33
  complex patterns of, 143
  models, 140
  pattern, 121, 133-34
    factors determining, 135

Wade, 127
Waller, Robert, 88
Walter, Deblie, 88
Waves, 134,135
Wober, Mallory, 83
Wobblers/floaters, 14, 54
Women audience, 57, 58

Yadav, J.S., 8,9
Younger politicians, 32, 33, 36, 39